Eat Your Greens!

We've heard it said so many times. Here, Pete Evans makes eating green easy, with more than 130 mouth-watering dishes that take veggies from sides to stars.

Even the pickiest eater will be won over by crispy carrot fritters with garlicky yoghurt dipping sauce, oh-so-simple sweet potato waffles topped with guacamole and a fried egg or the oozy deliciousness that is eggplant parmigiana.

Eat Your Greens also includes simple tips on:

—increasing your family's veg intake for breakfast, lunch and dinner

—buying and growing seasonal, organic produce

—harnessing the health benefits of different veggies.

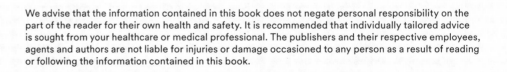

New ways to celebrate vegetables with
more than 130 easy plant-based recipes

Eat Your GREENS

PETE EVANS

plum. Pan Macmillan Australia

This book is dedicated to all the parents, children, grandparents, school teachers, guardians, farmers and gardeners who either love their veggies or are looking for new ways to celebrate the amazing and wide variety of vegetables we have the privilege of cooking and preparing for ourselves and our loved ones. Keep cooking with love and laughter, and celebrating the empowerment of wise choices.

INTRODUCTION

Since my wife, Nic, and I moved to a farm a few years ago we've had the privilege of getting up close and personal with plants and nature. We've learned about seasonal rhythms and how to grow and cook our own fruit and vegetables and eat sustainably and ethically. My desire to encourage you to eat your veggies and really celebrate them at meal times, so they are the foundation of any plate, is what inspired me to write this book. Also, I wanted to share the valuable knowledge we've picked up along the way and celebrate our abundance of in-season vegetables with recipes we've created with you, your family and friends in mind.

At its core the paleo lifestyle embraces a plant-based diet, making vegetables a hero of every meal. A main component of each meal we eat should be veggies – particularly non-starchy ones – as they are packed full of vitamins and minerals, and are our only source of phytonutrients (the health-boosting compounds produced by plants that are responsible for their vibrant colours).

However, plant foods don't contain every vitamin and mineral we need for good health, and there are many nutrients that are much more easily and efficiently obtained by eating animal proteins and fats. For example, spinach may contain protein, but nowhere near as much as you'd find in beef, and vitamin B12 can only be obtained from animal products. So the idea behind paleo is a simple one, but one that many seem to overlook in the health space: to fill your plate at every meal with gorgeous in-season vegetables, then add a modest serving of sustainably sourced good-quality protein (think seafood, beef, lamb, chicken, venison, eggs and more), a side of fermented vegetables and include some bone broth for great gut health.

I believe eating vegetables shouldn't be a struggle for any of us. I love to eat whatever seasonal, anti-inflammatory plant life Mother Nature chooses to provide. While I firmly remain an omnivore (eating plants and meat/seafood/eggs), because it gives me the full range of nutrients I need to survive and thrive, my main motivation is to eat well so that I'm happy and fit enough to live a long and fruitful life. I joke with my kids that I will still be surfing when I am 100 years old!

Over the last few years a plant-based revolution has gained a lot of traction. More and more people are eating and enjoying a wider variety of veggies because they are not only delicious but extremely versatile too. As a chef, that gets me really excited. There are just so many inventive ways you can eat your greens. And at any meal, plant-based dishes can be the main star or the supporting act. The changing seasons give us the opportunity to make the most of the comings and goings of different types of fruit and vegetables by transforming them into dishes that nourish and support us – body, mind and soul – as well as the environment we live in.

There are many reasons why eating a predominantly plant-based diet is important. Not just for the health of us as humans but also for the planet – and its survival. Nutritionally, low-carb fruit and veggies are game-changers. We know that eating lots of leafy green veggies is something we need to encourage and celebrate at meal times. They are full of vitamins, minerals and polyphenols (micronutrients) and are rich in phytonutrients, phytochemicals and antioxidants that are essential for wellbeing. Among them are the most nutrient-dense food sources available.

With that in mind, we all need to consider the following:

— How do you like to eat your veggies?
— Do you eat enough veggies every week?
— Do you grow your own fruit and veggies?
— Do you buy them from your local farmers' market or organic co-op? Or do you buy them from the supermarket?
— If someone else grows your fruit and veggies, do you know how they're farmed – whether they've been planted and harvested in a way that nurtures, not robs, the earth?
— Do you know what they've been sprayed with before they appear on your plate?

Interestingly, because of their medicinal properties, every culture in the world includes greens in its diet in some way. In Japan, bitter greens (such as tatsoi) are eaten for their ability to increase bile and build a stronger digestive system. Meanwhile, in Maori culture, puha – a dark green plant often found growing as a weed and traditionally served with meat and seafood – is known for its bitterness and life-sustaining properties.

Never has there been a more important time for humans to step up and find a way to live in harmony with the plant life on this planet. You see, there has always been a symbiotic relationship between humans, animals and plants. And, if nurtured in the right way, plants and grasslands can help us improve the health of the earth, rebuild topsoil and feed us and animals in far more sustainable and holistic ways.

It's all about the actions we take and the choices we make – from what we buy at the supermarket, to what food we put on our plates and grow in our gardens (no matter how big or small), every decision needs to nurture our planet. We can support the producers who are farming the land in ethical, sustainable ways. This means doing a bit of research, knowing the source of our food and being wise about where we spend our money and the farmers and/or companies we choose to support. Simply put, growing more plants, eating more plants and honouring the cycle of life should be beneficial for us and the earth.

It all comes down to this: the sun, plants and grasslands (the homes of herbivores), our waterways and oceans, as well as the air we breathe, are at the heart of everything and are a necessary part of life as we know it. They produce and degrade. They help us build healthy soil. They provide a rich array of nutrients for all life: animals and us.

I firmly believe that if we commit to living in a kind, compassionate and responsible way, while working together to find sustainable solutions that allow us to live in balance, we can bring about positive change. And this need not seem insurmountable. We can all make a difference by reducing waste, reusing, recycling, growing our own greens, supporting our local farmers and composting. We can all find new ways to be part of the regeneration of our precious planet.

Thank you once again for your trust and commitment. I am so happy that I get to share more recipes to inspire you to cook up a healthy and delicious storm in your kitchen. I hope this book truly makes your mealtimes a celebration of the seasonal abundance of the fruit and veggies that enrich your daily experiences.

Cook with love and laughter,

Pete Evans

V IS FOR
VEGGIES

I want to inspire you to make the most of the plant power revolution and be bold, brave and beautiful with your vegetable choices. The next time you choose to chow down on plants, think about how there is so much more to each and every veggie than just their amazing flavour; it's also about recognising their nutritional qualities and the role they play in digestion. When you consume a vegetable, your stomach breaks it down and then uses the nutrients to feed different parts of your body. These nutrients help your blood circulate, keep your central nervous system functioning and balance your immune system so it can fight off disease.

Eating different types of fruit, herbs and veggies provides us with different nutrients and helps us to absorb them. That's why we all need to embrace a wide, colourful array of in-season fruit and veggies when we eat. And that may be as simple as eating one type of vegetable or as elaborate as a combination of different low-carb fruit, herbs and vegetables at each meal.

Take, for instance, beetroot versus spinach. Beetroot is a root vegetable made up of deeply concentrated minerals and vitamins, which become denser as the vegetable grows beneath the ground. By contrast, spinach, which grows above ground, is watered by the rain and expands and contracts in response to the heat of the day and the cool of the night. Beetroot contains potassium, magnesium and iron, vitamins A, B6 and C, folic acid, antioxidants and fibre, and its leaves are a good source of calcium, iron, beta-carotene and vitamin C; spinach contains folic acid, calcium, iron, potassium and magnesium, as well as vitamins A, B2, C and K, carotenes and the antioxidant lutein.

We all need to embrace a wide, colourful array of in-season fruit and veggies when we eat.

Just like when we build a house, we need the foundations (our digestive, immune and nervous systems and mitochondria) to be strong, versatile and adaptable to withstand any storm or damage. Eating a wide variety of fruit and vegetables, alongside well-sourced animal protein and fat, is the most effective way to do this as they give our bodies the building blocks (vitamins, minerals, antioxidants, essential amino acids, etc.) we need to make sure our base is rock-solid. They provide the necessary nutrients we need to do everything from getting the right balance of bacteria in our guts to protecting our cells against harmful invaders.

PLANT POWER

Let me introduce you to a whole new world of plants that are good for your health and delicious for your palate. So, how do you know which plant foods to choose? I encourage you to eat as many colours of the low-carb vegetable, fruit and herb rainbow as you can, as well as some higher-carb veggies and fruit one or two days per week (with the exception of white potatoes). Be careful not to eat a mountain of sweet potato with every meal as it can raise your blood-sugar levels, which is what we're trying to avoid with a plant-based paleo approach. When you can't grow your own produce, wherever your budget allows, select good-quality biodynamic, spray-free or organic produce. The mass-produced varieties sold in supermarkets tend to be less nutrient-dense, as they've been cultivated over time to be larger, sweeter and more homogenous-looking at the expense of taste, variety and nutritional value.

If your budget doesn't extend to buying all organic fruit and veg, check out the Environmental Working Group's annual Dirty Dozen and Clean 15 for a list of what fruit and vegetables to buy and what to avoid. The EWG is an American health and environmental research body that measures which fruit and vegetables are the most (and least) likely to contain pesticide residue. The lists vary from year to year, but provide a good quick reference.

Develop your own sense of taste and listen to your body, as this is the best way to identify what fruit and vegetables nourish you the most. Cravings for a certain type of fruit or vegetable may indicate that your body needs those particular nutrients. Being aware in this way will help you take control of your own nutrition. For instance, I can't help picking the cucumbers growing in our veggie garden at home the moment they're ready and enjoying every mouthful within minutes of harvesting them; the same can be said for herbs and other leafy greens from our patch.

These are 10 important nutrients that you can generally only get from plant foods:

1. Beta-glucan

One of the most widely studied types of fibre, beta-glucan is an effective prebiotic, which improves colon health. It may also help to lower blood pressure and keep blood-sugar levels stable by reducing the rate at which the small intestine absorbs simple sugars. Mushrooms, seaweeds and dates are good sources of beta-glucan.

2. Catechins

Catechins are a family of flavonoids, the most common group of antioxidants in plants. They are found in many plant-based foods and beverages, such as sweet potato, berries, cacao, pears, grapes, apples and green and black tea.

3. Cyanidin

Cyanidin is an anthocyanin – the antioxidant pigments that are responsible for the bright colours of many fruit and vegetables. It has a role to play in cardiovascular health, as well as strengthening bones. Good sources include berries, grapes, olives and cacao.

4. Hesperidin

This is a common flavanone – a type of flavonoid – known for its aromatic properties. Some studies have researched the role of hesperidin in preventing heart disease and cancer. Good sources are broccoli, green capsicums, parsley and citrus fruits, such as oranges, grapefruits and lemons.

5. Inulin

Inulin is a prebiotic fibre that belongs to a group known as fructans. It stimulates the growth of beneficial bacteria and helps the colon to function correctly, by reducing constipation and improving gut health. Some studies have also found that it aids calcium absorption and suppresses hunger. Sources of inulin include asparagus, onions, garlic, Jerusalem artichokes, fresh herbs, bananas and leeks.

6. Lignans

Lignans are polyphenols (plant micronutrients) that ferment in the intestines and are converted to phytoestrogens, which have been linked to a lower risk of heart disease and cancer. A good source is seeds, especially flaxseeds, as well as vegetables and berries.

7. Pectin

This is another prebiotic fibre found in fruit. It is excellent at moderating blood-sugar levels after meals and some studies suggest pectin may help prevent colon cancer. Carrots, tomatoes, peas, oranges, apples, grapefruit and peaches are all great sources of pectin.

8. Quercetin

This compound is another one of the flavonoids, the most common group of antioxidants in plants. High levels of quercetin have been linked to lower inflammation and blood pressure, and reduced risk of heart disease. Sources include spinach, kale, broccoli, cabbage, tomatoes, citrus fruits, apples, capers and onions.

9. Resistant starch

The most common type of carbohydrates in plant foods are starches. Resistant starch is a type of starch that is difficult to digest and passes through the stomach and small intestine to the large intestine intact. It promotes gut health by fermenting and feeding beneficial bacteria in the colon. It also helps us feel full for longer and limits the amount of sugar absorbed in the bloodstream after a meal. Green mango, green papaya and green bananas, as well as cooked and cooled sweet potato and other root vegetables, are good sources of resistant starch. I don't go overboard with resistant starch, but like to include a little in my diet every week.

10. Vitamin C

We are completely dependent on getting this vitamin from our food. Vitamin C is important for the immune system and for building connective tissue in the body. It is also a powerful antioxidant. Most plant foods contain vitamin C. Citrus fruits are an excellent source, as are broccoli, cauliflower, brussels sprouts, kale, parsley, capsicums and Kakadu plums. Interestingly, vitamin C is also present in beef liver.

PLANT SUPERSTARS

So, what plant foods should you be eating a whole lot more of?
Here's a handy table of nutrient-dense superstar fruit, vegetables
and herbs that I like to include in my diet when they are in season.

Kale	Broccoli	Broccolini	Watercress	Green beans
Parsley	Rocket	Spinach	Snow peas	Asparagus
Brussels sprouts	Kohlrabi	Spring onions	Bok choy	Cucumbers
Fennel	Leeks	Artichokes	Sprouts	Lettuce
Avocado	Silverbeet	Choy sum	Mustard greens	Celery
Okra	Limes	Lemons	Capsicum	Shallots
Carrots	Oranges	Pumpkin	Tomatoes	Strawberries
Chillies	Grapefruit	Radishes	Rhubarb	Eggplant
Onions	Blueberries	Garlic	Cauliflower	Cabbage

Note: people with autoimmune disease may need to eliminate nightshades such as chilli, tomato, capsicum, eggplant, goji berries and white potato, as they can be inflammatory. Some people may also react to garlic, onion and leek. As always, any food sensitivity testing or significant dietary change should be overseen by a healthcare professional.

Develop your own
sense of taste and
listen to your body,
as this is the best
way to identify what
fruit and vegetables
nourish you the most.

EXPAND YOUR PLANT POWER

One of my main goals in writing this book was to find ways to make people think more broadly about the types of plant life they eat and to start including some of the most nutrient-dense foods in the world, known for their ability to help us age gracefully and live well.

Here are a few plants I suggest you try to expand your plant power and rev up your life.

Eat as many colours of the low-carb vegetable, fruit and herb rainbow as you can, and when you can't grow your own, wherever your budget allows, select good-quality biodynamic, spray-free or organic ones.

Adaptogenic herbs

Adaptogens are herbs that balance the body to help it adapt to physical, chemical and environmental stresses. Many have antidepressant and anti-anxiety effects. Including them in your diet can help you deal with stress and burnout. They are excellent steeped in hot water to drink as a tea or try including them in a smoothie. My favourite adaptogens are holy basil (tulsi), licorice root and Indian ginseng (ashwagandha).

Bitter foods

Eating bitter foods helps to stimulate digestion and bile production. Bitterness can also expand the palate and help to stop sweet cravings. Lemons, limes, grapefruit, rocket, radicchio, chicory, witlof, endive, dandelion leaves and artichoke are all great to include in your diet to really get your digestion pumping.

Edible flowers

Edible flowers are an excellent addition to spring and summer dishes and can be used as a taste sensation to decorate salads, side dishes, main courses and desserts. Flowers from herbs such as garlic chives and coriander can add extra depth to dishes, while edible flowers such as borage and nasturtium can add particular flavours, such as cucumber and pepper, respectively.

Hemp

Food Standards Australia New Zealand (FSANZ) has recently changed the law to allow hemp-based food products to be sold. I think everyone should look at including hemp in their diet in some way. Studies have shown the consumption of raw hemp seeds can help improve digestive health, lower blood pressure, improve the immune system, control blood-sugar levels and minimise inflammation. Hemp seeds are a complete protein (meaning they contain all the essential amino acids our bodies can't produce) and a good source of vitamins and minerals with an excellent balance of omega-3 and omega-6 fatty acids.

Native Australian ingredients

We live on one of the harshest continents on the planet, so it's not surprising that this land has produced some of the most powerful superfoods in existence. Native bush tucker has some extraordinary medicinal qualities – think finger limes, Davidson plums, lemon myrtle, quandong, Kakadu plums, wattleseed, pepperberry, native seagrass, saltbush, and more. (One of my dreams is to release an all-native cookbook in the future, so watch this space! In the meantime, start experimenting with native ingredients – you may need to order online as they aren't always readily available in regular shops.)

Sea vegetables

Sea vegetables should have a regular place in our diet, as edible seaweed varieties are among the richest sources of iodine, magnesium, calcium, iron, zinc, potassium, manganese and all other minerals needed by the body. The most readily available is kelp and you can eat it in different ways – wild, fresh, dried or as noodles. Nori is another excellent, milder choice – wrap nori sheets around your salads or crumble into soups. Kombu, wakame, dulse and spirulina also make excellent additions to your diet.

JOIN
THE FOOD
REVOLUTION

Food is a basic right for all of us, but we need to look more closely at where our food comes from and how much we waste. Whether it's making organic choices that support sustainable farming, choosing renewable energy over fossil fuels, growing our own vegetables, fruit and herbs or reducing, recycling, reusing and – wherever possible – composting so that we create as little waste as possible, we all need to recognise that every step we take, no matter how small, has an impact. It is time to honour the life cycle of plants and animals by making conscious choices that support the health of our planet – and ultimately us. Live lightly, tread quietly, eat organically and give back to Mother Nature wherever and whenever you can.

BE THE SOLUTION

If we want to be part of the solution and bring about change, we have to be honest with ourselves about the origins of our food. Imagine if we all did our bit to influence the way the world's food chain operates. We can turn it from an industrialised one that's focused solely on capital gain to one where justice, responsibility and welfare are just as important as profit.

When it comes to the vegetables you consume, it's about choosing ones that haven't been grown commercially with damaging synthetic fertilisers to increase pest-resistance and super-charge growth rates. Instead, buy holistically farmed organic or spray-free fruit and veg and select in season.

When it comes to buying seasonal fresh produce, there are no hard and fast rules. Australia has different climatic regions – cool, temperate, subtropical and tropical – and what is in season will vary depending on where you live. The best way to find out what fruit and veg is in season is to shop at your local greengrocer, farmers' market or wholefood store and get to know the people you're buying from. They'll be happy to talk to you and share what they know. When buying from a supermarket choose local and biodynamic or organic; limit or reject imported fruit and veg, as this usually means it is out of season.

Ask questions, do some research and support producers who grow food in a sustainable and ethical way that nurtures the health of the air and soil.

We should all try to get involved and take responsibility for our role in the global food chain. Why not have a go at growing your own organic vegetables? Try planting fresh herbs and salad leaves in window boxes or in pots on the balcony of your inner-city apartment, dig a patch in your backyard, join a community garden or farm larger plots of land. (Check out Planting for a Healthy Planet on page 20 for handy hints on how to start a veggie garden.) Having your own garden and shopping at your local farmers' market means you can live and eat with the seasons in a way that supports nature. Will you join me in being part of the solution?

PLANTING FOR A
HEALTHY PLANET

We humans are just one small part of the vibrant, interrelated communities of plants and bacteria that live on our planet. Without plants and bacteria, humans, animals and the soil that wraps itself round the earth like a nurturing coat will cease to exist and there will be no life.

SOIL QUALITY COUNTS

The place where all plant life springs from starts with what's beneath our feet – our soil. There is a whole living world down there that we can all learn how to nurture.

We have to give back because the soil is alive. Alive with a million living things – all doing what they can to make the planet liveable by breaking down dead matter from plants, animals, fungi and bacteria and providing nutrients for plants.

Soil conservation really matters. The quality of our soil ensures food security for all of us. When plants take over bare soil, the soil is able to absorb and hold water, to store carbon and to break down methane. But when soil is bare, with no plants to bind it, it is simply washed or blown away. And if topsoil is damaged, it gives off carbon, which contributes to the problem.

Soil is the building block of life. We need to recognise its importance and support only improved food practices that sustainably manage soil, water, crops, livestock and other components of farming systems. We need to ensure food stability through reliable agronomic production that addresses climate change and ensures food access for all.

If we all take charge of our own microclimates, together we can have a positive impact on our global macroclimate. And one way we can do this is by cultivating plants in a holistic manner in conjunction with holistic animal-farming practices.

POLYCULTURES

The easiest way to understand polycultures is to think about the plant and animal interactions that happen when nature is left to do its thing. For example, think of a native forest, prairie or wetlands. Every part is a symphony of plants, microfauna (bacteria, yeasts and fungi), insects and animals all interconnected and working together to create a community. This delicate dance of interconnection forms the cornerstones of permaculture.

Permaculture takes a holistic approach to resource and land management, meaning we can plant and farm in ways that support species diversity to create healthy, thriving ecosystems.

What if we all applied these principles to our own backyards or if our local grocery store sourced all of its food from farmers who put these principles into practice? Imagine the ripple effect it would have on our global food economy. (For more information on permaculture, check out Milkwood in Australia and Polyface Farms and the Savory Institute in the US.)

GROWING ORGANIC FRUIT AND VEGETABLES

One of the best ways to celebrate fruit and vegetables is by growing your own. It's a process I've been learning over the last few years, and now I know from experience that nothing is more satisfying than picking seasonal greens you've grown with your own hands.

Planting trees and growing our own food are small worthwhile contributions that we can all make for the health of our planet. And I reckon it's the core of a healthy lifestyle, too.

Getting down and dirty out in the garden with our children is a great way to show them where our food comes from and it also helps them appreciate nature, its amazing bounty and the environment. Kids love digging, planting and watering. Adults too. In fact, I've been more inspired than ever to cook with plants since I've had my own veggie garden. Heading outside and checking out what's in season provides me with massive amounts of motivation for what I'm going to create next in the kitchen.

Imagine what would happen if everyone in Australia turned a little bit of earth into a bed of veggies or planted a citrus tree in the backyard. Imagine if those vegetables weren't sprayed with any nasties and were grown in soil that's free from synthetic fertilisers and pesticides. Imagine the amount of beneficial bugs that would stick around and do the job nature intended.

On top of all that, getting our hands and feet dirty in the garden, amongst all that good bacteria–rich soil, has positive health benefits for adults and children, as paediatric neurologist Dr Maya Shetreat-Klein demonstrates in her book *The Dirt Cure*.

So, while I'm a chef first and foremost, these are the reasons why I've included this chapter on gardening. I now know when it comes to preparing food, there is simply nothing better and nothing fresher or more nutrient-packed than eating fruit and vegetables you've picked and grown yourself in your own patch of soil.

WHAT GROWS WHERE YOU LIVE?

When it comes to putting a veggie garden on your patch, I urge everyone to ask this one small question: what grows where you live?

By understanding what plants grow best in your area, you can work out how to honour the cycle of life by planting fruit trees, herbs and vegetables that best suit your environment.

Sure, it's about the seasons and understanding their rhythms, but it's also about planting annuals and perennials that flourish – and have always flourished – in your area. And then learning how to grow them in a way that helps rebuild topsoil and takes care of the planet, year after year.

Planting trees and growing our own food are small worthwhile contributions that we can all make for the health of our planet.

I know from my own experience that edible gardens create abundance. Our vegetable garden is often overflowing with produce and we have no choice but to pickle and preserve. It only takes a good freezer, a few great recipes, some storage containers and half a day on the weekend and your family's meals will be sorted for months to come. The other really awesome thing about having a flourishing garden that produces pesticide-free vegetables is that you can trade your surplus homegrown produce with others in your local community.

UNDERSTANDING ORGANIC FARMING

The reason I support organic farming and farm organically myself is because it's a way to recycle resources and create an environment that nurtures balanced, healthy ecosystems.

Organic farming is about conserving biodiversity. It's about steering clear of synthetic pesticides and fertilisers that do nothing good for our health, or the health of the earth. The principles of organic farming are easy to understand. Organic farming is about knowing your source and understanding that the food you are eating is grown in a way that means it tastes great and is great for you and the plant's growth cycle.

It only takes a good freezer, a few great recipes, some storage containers and half a day on the weekend and your family's meals will be sorted for months to come.

Permaculture is another step forward again. When we use permaculture practices to grow our food, we design our gardens and our farms to mimic nature's powerful patterns and relationships. It's about humans and animals integrating with their environment to create healthy, productive places that day after day, year after year, build topsoil and nurture the earth so that it is allowed to give back with abundance.

Whether you apply permaculture practices to a raised garden bed in your backyard or to an entire farm, you will be making sure that every time you plant something, you are creating biodiversity. This means your soil becomes healthier, your plants are more resilient and everything grows more easily, with minimal effort.

YOUR OWN EDIBLE GARDEN

Growing your own organic fruit and vegetables is an awesome way to provide your family with a variety of in-season foods; and if you plan your garden well, get a bit of expert help to kickstart your green thumb and stagger out planting so it's manageable, it can also end up being really good for your budget.

There are plenty of businesses out there to help you get set up, regardless of how much or little space you have. Raised garden beds are a great option for small, inner-city properties – and you don't need any space at all to grow herbs and chillies in pots on the balcony or windowsill!

We have a few raised garden beds at our place now, and use permaculture practices to grow a great range of edibles. The beds are made from untreated sustainable cypress timber and are filled to the brim with all the ingredients needed to create rich and nutritious soil. Some of these include seaweed, rock minerals, organic mushroom compost, molasses, cow dung and lots, lots more. This not only ensures the right balance of nutrients but the healthy soil means it can hold up to three times more water than normal soil, and that means less watering, which is especially important for areas of Australia that are prone to drought.

I consider myself a pretty confident gardener these days. To help kickstart your own garden journey, I want to share my five easy steps to creating the perfect edible garden:

1. Start small

I began by planting a few leafy greens and some of my favourite herbs – thyme, rosemary and parsley – in my first garden bed, which I deliberately put close to the kitchen. This meant it was close for picking ingredients and also for keeping an eye on the plants.

2. Grow to ratios

When I'm choosing what to grow, I think about the time it will take and how much I'll get when I harvest. I've learned by trial and error. For example, big brassicas such as broccoli and cabbage take a lot of space to grow and a lot of time to mature. And then, when they are almost ready to pick, they are often gobbled up by pests like white caterpillar. That's why I make sure most of my patch includes other greens, such as lettuce, silverbeet, watercress, mustard cress, mustard leaf, endive and kale, that I can easily pick and eat and that will regenerate quickly.

3. Mulch

Whenever vegetables grow in soil, they use up the available nutrients to ensure they grow as strong as possible. So it's really important to have good-quality nutritiously rich soil. The other key point is to make sure you mulch around your vegetables, especially before summer. Mulching helps to retain moisture and add more nutrients to the soil so you can water your garden less. I like to use tea tree mulch or sugar cane mulch because it looks tidy but you can also use fallen leaves or lawn clippings. Just make sure you leave a decent amount of space around the roots of the vegetables; taking mulch all the way up to the stem can cause your veggies to rot.

4. Eat straight out of the patch

When you first start your vegetable garden, it's like having a bunch of miracles happening outside your kitchen door almost every night, especially when it's an abundant season, such as summer. I love nothing more than going outside and crunching on a leafy green straight out of the garden. Nothing tastes better than when you grow it yourself.

5. If you have space, plant your first citrus tree

Once I'd mastered my first veggie patch, I planted a lemon tree and a finger lime tree. Lemon and other types of citrus trees are best planted in spring or early summer because they mature during winter. I'm pretty proud of the lemons my tree produces and feel stoked every time I get a new fruit. Citrus trees are perennials, so they keep producing for years to come and are great for your soil. Plus, having citrus on hand, basically for free, to squeeze into a glass of water or over a piece of fish is bloody awesome!

Taking baby steps like this has allowed my garden to evolve naturally and, now, there's a whole edible world just outside our kitchen that Nic and I are creating. As with cooking, gardening is about experimenting with different varieties and flavours to obtain the optimum balance. Most of all, we love teaching my girls, Chilli and Indii, where food comes from and how to look after it.

FROM GARDEN TO TABLE

I encourage everyone who wants to live well and cook well to grow your own healthy produce and take it from garden to table. Having a garden is a really cool way to bring yourself back down to earth. Being outside, enjoying the soil and sunshine and getting your hands dirty is the ultimate way to chill out, relax and have more abundance in your life. And I hope the recipes that follow will provide you with all the inspiration you need to cook up a storm with the fruits and vegetables of your labours.

Breakfast

Pumpkin Spice Latte/ Hemp Bircher/ Mushroom Latte/
Chilli and Indii's Jelly Slice/ Spiced Pumpkin Pancakes/
Beetroot Latte/ Dr Mercola's Avocado Fat Bomb/ Carrot
Fritters with Garlic and Yoghurt Sauce/ Avocado on
Toast with Macadamia 'Cheese'/ Baked Eggs with
Tomato/ Grilled Broccoli Steak with Fried Egg and
Romesco Sauce/ Sweet Potato Waffles with Guacamole
and Fried Egg/ Broccoli Omelette/ Silverbeet and Kale
Shakshuka/ Parsnip and Zucchini Hash Browns/
Japanese Pancakes/ Pumpkin and Silverbeet Broth
with Cauliflower Rice/ Zoodle and Veg Pikelets

Serves 2

Mmmm, on a chilly day who can resist a deliciously comforting and nourishing pumpkin spice latte? The key, of course, is the harmonious blend of spices that tantalise the tastebuds and warm the soul. For a summer treat, you could serve a chilled version of this as a smoothie or freeze it in popsicle moulds to make icy poles.

PUMPKIN SPICE LATTE

350 ml coconut, hemp or nut milk
100 g Pumpkin Puree (page 322)
maple syrup, honey or a couple
    of drops of liquid stevia,*
    to taste (optional)
2 shots of espresso or 250 ml (1 cup)
    freshly brewed coffee

Pumpkin pie spice
2 tablespoons ground cinnamon
1 tablespoon ground ginger
1 teaspoon ground allspice
½ teaspoon ground cloves
¼ teaspoon freshly grated nutmeg
pinch of ground turmeric

* See Glossary

To make the pumpkin pie spice, combine all the ingredients in a small bowl and mix together with a fork. (Makes about 35 g.)

In a small saucepan over medium–low heat, whisk together the milk, pumpkin puree, ½ teaspoon of pumpkin pie spice and the sweetener of your choice, if desired. Continue to whisk constantly until the mixture just starts to come to a simmer or is hot to touch. Remove from the heat and carefully pour into a blender. Blend for 20 seconds, or until frothy.

Meanwhile, pour the coffee into two latte glasses or cups. Top each glass or cup with the hot pumpkin milk and sprinkle with some extra pumpkin pie spice. Serve.

Store the remaining pumpkin pie spice in a clean spice jar with a lid for up to 3 months.

Notes
– If using coconut milk and you find your pumpkin spice latte a little too creamy, stir through some boiling water to reach your desired consistency.
– You can use a milk frother instead of a blender for blending your spiced pumpkin latte.

Serves 2

Hemp seeds – the heart of the hemp plant, *Cannabis sativa* – are becoming increasingly popular, and for good reason. They are incredibly nutritious and have an excellent 3:1 balance of omega-3 and omega-6 fatty acids, which promote cardiovascular health, and are high in GLA, an essential omega-6 fatty acid that's been proven to balance hormones. They are also a perfect protein, containing all 20 amino acids, including the nine essential amino acids that our bodies can't produce. Why not add them to your diet in a very simple way with this delicious bircher muesli?

HEMP BIRCHER

55 g (½ cup) hemp seeds,
    plus extra to serve
1 tablespoon chia seeds
2 tablespoons flaxseeds
¼ teaspoon ground cinnamon,
    plus extra to serve
¼ teaspoon vanilla powder or paste
125 g (½ cup) Coconut Yoghurt
    (page 314), plus extra to serve
185 ml (¾ cup) almond or coconut milk
1 green apple, grated
sweetener of your choice (such as liquid
    stevia* or honey), to taste (optional)
fresh or frozen blueberries, to serve

* See Glossary

You'll need to begin this recipe a day ahead.

Place the hemp seeds, chia seeds, flaxseeds, cinnamon, vanilla, coconut yoghurt and almond or coconut milk in a bowl and mix well to combine. Cover and refrigerate overnight.

The next morning, mix through the grated apple and sweetener of your choice, if desired, and spoon the bircher into two serving bowls or jars. Top with some extra yoghurt, the blueberries, some extra hemp seeds and a little extra cinnamon. Alternatively, layer it up as we've done here.

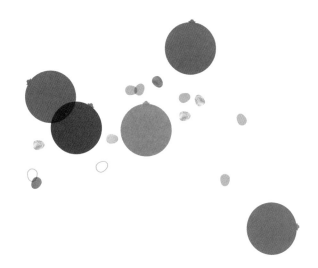

Serves 1

Mushrooms are truly one of nature's most wonderful and magical treasures. We are still learning about their healing properties, not only for our own bodies but also for the earth itself. Mushroom elixirs and powders are becoming more and more popular and I simply couldn't write a book about eating your veggies without including this very special ingredient. You can serve your latte hot or cold, depending on the time of year, and choose whatever non-dairy milk you love. Macadamia or cashew milk also work well.

MUSHROOM LATTE

250 ml (1 cup) coconut, hemp or nut milk
1 teaspoon mushroom powder
    (reishi, shiitake, lion's mane
    or a blend)*
¼ teaspoon ground cinnamon
1–2 drops of liquid stevia*
    or sweetener of your
    choice (optional)
1 teaspoon MCT oil* or coconut oil
    (optional)

* See Glossary

Combine all the ingredients in a small saucepan and stir well. Place over low heat and, while slowly stirring, gently heat until hot.

Transfer the hot latte mixture to a blender. Blend on low, working up to high speed for 1 minute, or until foamy. Pour the mixture into a latte glass or a mug and enjoy.

Notes
– If using coconut milk and you find your mushroom latte a little too creamy, stir through some boiling water to reach your desired consistency.
– You can use a milk frother instead of a blender for blending your mushroom latte.

Makes up to 40 serves
(depending on the size
of the slices)

Nic and I have been making this slice for Chilli and Indii for years. It is one of the most frequently requested dishes in our home! This slice uses aloe vera juice and blueberry probiotic liquid as the base to add flavour and probiotic goodness. Alternatively, you can omit them and make a simple blueberry jelly slice.

CHILLI AND INDII'S JELLY SLICE

60 g powdered gelatine*
300 ml coconut water
155 g (1 cup) frozen blueberries, thawed
3 tablespoons lemon juice
80 ml (⅓ cup) aloe vera juice* (optional)
2 tablespoons concentrated blueberry probiotic liquid* (or any probiotic liquid or powder of your choice) (optional)
fresh berries, to serve

* See Glossary

Grease a 20 cm × 10 cm loaf tin.

Sprinkle the gelatine over 300 ml of cold water, mix well and stand for at least 5 minutes to allow the gelatine granules to expand and soften.

Place the coconut water and blueberries in a small saucepan and bring to a simmer over medium–low heat. Stir in the gelatine mixture and continue to stir for 2 minutes, or until the gelatine is completely dissolved. Remove from the heat and stir in the lemon juice.

Pour the blueberry mixture into a blender and blend until smooth. Strain through a fine sieve into a jug or bowl. (Discard the leftover blueberry pulp.) Allow the mixture to cool to lukewarm (34–36°C), then stir in the aloe vera juice and probiotic (if using). (Remember: probiotics contain beneficial live bacteria, which will be destroyed if added to hot liquid or food.) Immediately pour the jelly mixture into the prepared tin, cover and place in the fridge to set for 1 hour, or until firm.

Remove the jelly loaf from the tin, slice and serve with the fresh berries.

This slice will keep in an airtight container in the fridge for up to 2 weeks or in the freezer for up to 3 months (thaw before serving).

Serves 2–3

Pancakes have evolved over the decades. I made my first-ever pancake at home at about the age of 13; fast forward over 30 years and they now come in all shapes and sizes. The old-school plain or self-raising flour has been replaced with non-inflammatory ingredients like coconut flour and nut and seed flours. These pancakes use pumpkin in the batter to give it a good kick of nutrition. I think we have a lot more fun with ingredients these days.

SPICED PUMPKIN PANCAKES

150 g Pumpkin Puree (page 322)
5 eggs
80 ml (⅓ cup) nut milk
100 g (1 cup) almond meal
2 tablespoons coconut flour
2 tablespoons maple syrup
2 teaspoons baking powder
1 teaspoon ground cinnamon,
    plus extra to serve
1 teaspoon ground ginger
¼ teaspoon ground cardamom
pinch of sea salt
coconut oil, for cooking

To serve
Whipped Coconut Cream
    (page 323)
maple syrup
fresh blueberries

Place the pumpkin puree in a large bowl and add the eggs, nut milk, almond meal, coconut flour, maple syrup, baking powder, cinnamon, ginger, cardamom and salt. Stir with a whisk to combine.

Heat a tablespoon of coconut oil in a frying pan over medium–low heat. Working in batches of three or four, add 3 level tablespoons of batter per pancake and shape into rounds about 10 cm in diameter. Cook the pancakes for 1½ minutes, or until the underside is firm and starts to colour. Flip over and cook on the other side for 1 minute, or until lightly golden. Transfer to a warm plate. Repeat, adding more oil as necessary, until all the batter is used.

Pile the pancakes onto plates in stacks of three or four and serve with whipped coconut cream, maple syrup, blueberries and a dusting of cinnamon.

Serves 2

This latte, spiked with delicious spices, is a great way to include that awesome ingredient beetroot in your diet. Try out different types of milk and cream from nuts or seeds. In summer you might like to freeze this for yummy treats, such as icy poles or ice cream.

BEETROOT LATTE

400 ml coconut, hemp or nut milk
3 cardamom pods, lightly crushed
1 star anise, lightly crushed
1 cinnamon stick, lightly crushed
1 beetroot, grated
coconut sugar, honey or liquid
    stevia,* to taste

* See Glossary

Combine the milk, cardamom, star anise and cinnamon stick in a saucepan over medium–low heat. Bring to a gentle simmer, stir through the grated beetroot, then remove from the heat and set aside for 15 minutes to allow the flavours to develop. Reheat the beetroot milk over medium–low heat, stirring frequently until heated through.

Carefully strain the beetroot milk through a fine strainer into a blender, discarding the solids, then blend for 20 seconds, or until frothy. Pour into cups or latte glasses and stir in a little of your choice of sweetener, if desired.

Notes
– If using coconut milk and you find your beetroot latte a little too creamy, stir through some boiling water to reach your desired consistency.
– You can use a milk frother instead of a blender for blending your beetroot latte.

Serves 1–2

The old saying 'an apple a day keeps the doctor away' could very easily be improved upon by replacing apple with avocado! Over the last few years the low-fat diet approach has been well and truly debunked and a massive switch back to embracing good-quality fats – such as those found in avocados, nuts, coconut, wild-caught sustainable seafood, organic free-range eggs and grass-fed and finished meat – has started. This avocado fat bomb is a fabulous real-deal meal that provides proper nutrition to satisfy and nourish your body. This is a recipe from my dear friend and mentor, Dr Joseph Mercola.

DR MERCOLA'S AVOCADO FAT BOMB

1 tablespoon flaxseeds
1 tablespoon black sesame seeds
1 tablespoon chia seeds, plus extra to serve
1 tablespoon cumin seeds
600 ml filtered water, plus extra if needed
1 tablespoon psyllium husks*
1 tablespoon green superfood supplement of your choice
1 teaspoon calcium from ground-pastured eggs* (optional)
30 g cacao butter
1 avocado, halved, stone removed and peeled
1 tablespoon MCT oil*
1–4 drops of liquid stevia*
30–60 g fresh or frozen berries (optional)

* See Glossary

You'll need to begin this recipe a day ahead.

Combine the flaxseeds and sesame, chia and cumin seeds in a bowl with 500 ml (2 cups) of the filtered water and soak overnight (roughly 12 hours).

The next morning, drain the soaked seeds and place them in a high-speed blender. Pour in the remaining 100 ml of filtered water, add the remaining ingredients, except the berries, and blend until smooth. Add a little more water, if needed, until it reaches your desired consistency. The consistency can range from a liquid to a pudding texture, depending on how much water you add. Spoon into a serving bowl or two and sprinkle on the extra chia seeds. Serve with the berries, if desired.

Serves 2–4

My simple spiced carrot fritters are a nutritious replacement for the corn fritters so adored by Australians in the late '90s and early 2000s. I have teamed them with some chorizo because I just love using a little bit of fatty meat as a garnish to a vegetable dish like this. These make for amazing school or work lunch-box meals, so always make more than you think you will need.

CARROT FRITTERS WITH GARLIC AND YOGHURT SAUCE

500 g carrots, grated
sea salt and freshly ground
    black pepper
1 teaspoon ground cumin
1 teaspoon coriander seeds
1 tablespoon almond meal
    or coconut flour
1 tablespoon unhulled tahini
2 eggs
80 ml (⅓ cup) melted coconut
    oil or good-quality animal fat,*
    plus extra if needed
200 g chorizo sausage, chopped
    into 1 cm pieces (optional)

Garlic and yoghurt sauce
½ garlic clove, finely grated
150 g Coconut Yoghurt (page 314)
1½ teaspoons lemon juice
pinch of ground cumin

To serve
3 radishes, thinly sliced
1 handful of mint leaves
sesame seeds
lemon wedges

* See Glossary

Place the grated carrot in a colander, add 2 teaspoons of salt and mix well. Set aside for 15 minutes. Drain the liquid from the carrot and, using your hands, squeeze out as much excess moisture as possible.

Place the carrot, spices, almond meal or coconut flour, tahini and eggs in a bowl and mix to combine. Season with salt and pepper.

Heat half the oil or fat in a non-stick frying pan over medium heat. Cooking in batches of four, add 3 tablespoons of carrot mixture per fritter to the pan, flattening each with a spatula into 8 cm rounds. Cook for 2 minutes on each side, turning carefully, until golden. Place on paper towel to drain. Repeat with the remaining oil or fat and fritter mixture. Cover to keep warm.

Wipe the pan clean, add the chorizo and cook, stirring occasionally, over medium heat for 6–8 minutes, or until crisp.

Meanwhile, combine all the garlic and yoghurt sauce ingredients in a bowl and season with a pinch of salt.

Pile the fritters onto a serving plate, top with the chorizo, scatter on the radish and mint and sprinkle with sesame seeds. Serve with the garlic and yoghurt sauce and lemon wedges on the side.

Serves 4

I have been playing with versions of avocado on toast for the last 30 years – and it never gets boring. I always add some acid in the form of lemon or lime juice, vinegar, pickles, kraut or kimchi (this balances out the richness of the avo) and some heat in the form of pepper, chilli, wasabi, horseradish, ginger or garlic. Here, I've used toasted charcoal bread for the contrast in colour and macadamia 'cheese' to ramp up the good fats. Other great toppings include sliced tomato or radish, shredded rocket or radicchio, pickled red onion, smoked salmon or cooked prawns.

AVOCADO ON TOAST WITH MACADAMIA 'CHEESE'

240 g Macadamia 'Cheese'
     (page 320)
8 slices of Charcoal Bread
     (page 248) (see Note),
     lightly toasted
2 avocados, sliced
1 lemon, cut into wedges
2 tablespoons extra-virgin olive oil
sea salt and freshly ground
     black pepper
chilli flakes (optional)

Spread the macadamia 'cheese' over the toast. Arrange the avocado slices on top, then squeeze over a little lemon juice. Drizzle on the olive oil and season with salt and pepper and chilli flakes, if desired.

Note
– You could also use Macadamia Fat Bomb Bread (page 247), Nic's Amazing Hemp Bread (page 252) or any paleo bread of your choice.

Serves 4

Baked eggs with tomato – or eggs in purgatory – is a wonderful dish to prepare for any meal, whether it be a hearty breakfast, simple lunch or nourishing dinner. To up the nutritional profile, I add any greens that are growing in the garden. Here, I use silverbeet but you might like to try kale, spinach, radicchio or rainbow chard. You can also add any veggies that you love, such as mushrooms, roasted pumpkin or sweet potato, zucchini, broccoli, asparagus or, one of my favourites, okra.

BAKED EGGS WITH TOMATO

1 tablespoon coconut oil
    or good-quality animal fat*
1 onion, chopped
120 g bacon, chopped
4 garlic cloves, finely chopped
1 teaspoon ground cumin
1 teaspoon smoked paprika
½ teaspoon ground coriander
¼ teaspoon ground cinnamon
¼ teaspoon chilli flakes, or to taste
600 g diced tomatoes (see Note)
125 ml (½ cup) Chicken Bone
    Broth (page 312), vegetable
    stock or water
sea salt and freshly ground
    black pepper
½ bunch of silverbeet (about 120 g),
    stems removed and leaves torn
    (reserve stems for stocks and broths)
4 eggs
4 thin slices of Macadamia Fat
    Bomb Bread (page 247) or any
    paleo bread of your choice,
    lightly toasted

Herb oil
1 handful of coriander leaves, chopped,
    plus extra to serve (optional)
1 handful of flat-leaf parsley
    leaves, chopped
1 handful of dill fronds, chopped
½ teaspoon finely grated lemon zest
2 tablespoons apple cider vinegar
100 ml extra-virgin olive oil

* See Glossary

Preheat the oven to 180°C (160°C fan-forced).

Heat the oil or fat in a 21 cm heavy-based ovenproof pan over medium heat. Add the onion and bacon and cook, stirring occasionally, for about 5 minutes, or until softened and translucent. Stir in the garlic and spices and cook for about 30 seconds, or until fragrant.

Add the tomatoes and broth, stock or water to the pan and bring to the boil. Reduce the heat to low and simmer, stirring occasionally, for 10 minutes, or until the sauce has thickened. Season with salt and pepper and stir in the silverbeet leaves.

Using a spoon, create four small wells in the sauce and crack an egg into each well. Cover with a lid, then place in the oven for 15–18 minutes, or until the egg whites are set but the yolks are still runny.

Meanwhile, to make the herb oil, place all the ingredients in a bowl and mix to combine. Season with a little salt and pepper.

Season the egg yolks with salt and pepper and drizzle over the herb oil. Scatter over the extra coriander leaves, if using, and serve with the toast to mop up all the yummy juices.

Note
– I prefer to buy diced and whole peeled tomatoes in jars rather than cans, due to the presence of Bisphenol A (BPA) in some cans. BPA is a toxic chemical that can interfere with our hormonal system.

Serves 4

For me this dish epitomises what eating your greens is all about. To complement the broccoli, I have chosen the ever-versatile egg and teamed it with a romesco sauce. This has to be in the top ten sauces ever created. My version doesn't contain bread as it really doesn't need it, in my opinion. By omitting the bread, you have the perfect anti-inflammatory breakfast to enjoy.

GRILLED BROCCOLI STEAK WITH FRIED EGG AND ROMESCO SAUCE

sea salt and freshly ground
    black pepper
2 tablespoons coconut oil or
    good-quality animal fat*
1 large head of broccoli (about 400 g),
    cut lengthways into 4 pieces
    about 1.5 cm thick
4 eggs

Romesco sauce
2 red capsicums, quartered
2 tomatoes, quartered
1 long red chilli, halved, deseeded
    and sliced
1 teaspoon smoked paprika
1 rosemary sprig, leaves picked
    and finely chopped
1 tablespoon coconut oil, melted
12 hazelnuts (activated if possible*),
    lightly toasted
12 almonds (activated if possible*),
    lightly toasted
3 garlic cloves, crushed
2 tablespoons apple cider vinegar
80 ml (⅓ cup) olive oil

Hazelnut and garlic vinaigrette
60 g hazelnuts (activated if possible*),
    toasted and chopped
2 Garlic Confit cloves (page 318),
    chopped or mashed
1 tablespoon chopped flat-leaf
    or curly parsley
3 tablespoons olive oil
1 teaspoon apple cider vinegar

* See Glossary

Preheat the oven to 220°C (200°C fan-forced).

To make the romesco sauce, place the capsicum, skin-side up, on a baking tray and roast for 15–20 minutes, or until the skin blackens. Place the capsicum in a bowl, cover and set aside for 5 minutes to steam. Peel off the skin and remove the seeds, then chop the flesh and set aside.

Toss the tomato, chilli, paprika, rosemary and coconut oil in a bowl and season with salt and pepper. Heat a frying pan over medium heat, add the tomato mixture and cook for 3–4 minutes, or until soft.

Place the nuts in the bowl of a food processor and process until finely ground. Add the capsicum, the tomato and chilli mixture, the garlic and vinegar and process to a paste. With the motor running, slowly add the olive oil and blend until well combined. Taste and add more salt and pepper if necessary. Set aside until needed.

Reduce the oven to 180°C (160°C fan-forced). Line two baking trays with baking paper.

Melt 2 teaspoons of coconut oil or fat in a non-stick frying pan over medium–high heat. Add two broccoli steaks and cook, turning once, for 2 minutes, or until golden on each side. Transfer to one of the prepared trays and season with salt and pepper. Repeat this process with another 2 teaspoons of oil or fat and the remaining broccoli steaks. Place in the oven and roast for 18–22 minutes, or until the broccoli is tender.

Combine the vinaigrette ingredients in a bowl, season with salt and pepper and mix well.

Heat the remaining coconut oil or fat in a non-stick frying pan over medium heat. Fry the eggs for 2–3 minutes, or until cooked to your liking. Season, slide onto a plate and keep warm.

Spread 3–4 tablespoons of romesco sauce onto each serving plate. Place a broccoli steak on the sauce, then top with a fried egg. Drizzle over some vinaigrette, sprinkle with pepper and serve.

Tip
— Any leftover romesco sauce can
be stored in an airtight container
and refrigerated for up to 1 week.

Serves 2

I feel like this book is a bit of a classic hits album of dishes that have crossed over from the health-conscious to the mainstream public and become household names. One such dish, which burst onto the scene a few years ago, is sweet potato waffles. As an indulgent treat after a big surf, I love my waffles with a fried egg, bacon and a little maple syrup. For something lighter, I team them with guacamole, chilli and a fried egg. You can easily turn them into a dessert by adding fresh fruit and your favourite dairy-free ice cream or coconut yoghurt. Have a play around and enjoy the adventure.

SWEET POTATO WAFFLES
WITH GUACAMOLE AND FRIED EGG

sea salt and freshly ground
    black pepper
1 tablespoon coconut oil or
    good-quality animal fat,*
    plus extra for greasing
2 eggs
coriander leaves, to serve
chilli oil, to serve (optional)

Sweet potato waffles
300 g (about 1½ cups) peeled
    and grated sweet potato
3 eggs
1 tablespoon coconut flour
1 tablespoon coconut oil, melted
1 teaspoon baking powder

Simple guacamole
1 avocado, halved, stone removed
    and peeled
2 teaspoons lime juice,
    or to taste
1 teaspoon olive oil

* See Glossary

Preheat a waffle maker.

To make the guacamole, mash the avocado in a bowl and mix through the lime juice and olive oil. Season with salt and pepper and set aside.

To make the waffles, combine the sweet potato, eggs, coconut flour, coconut oil, baking powder, ¾ teaspoon of salt and ¼ teaspoon of pepper in a large bowl.

Generously grease the waffle maker hotplates. Spoon a quarter of the sweet potato mixture into the centre of the waffle iron. Close the lid and cook for 5–8 minutes, or until the waffle turns golden brown. Repeat with the remaining batter until you have four waffles.

Meanwhile, melt the oil or fat in a non-stick frying pan over medium heat. Crack the eggs into the pan and cook for 2–3 minutes, or until cooked to your liking. Season the eggs with salt and pepper.

Divide the waffles between two warm serving plates, then top with the guacamole, a fried egg and a sprinkle of coriander. Drizzle with the chilli oil, if desired.

Serves 2

There is no easier way to eat your greens than to add them to an omelette. This dish can break your fast or make for a speedy lunch or simple dinner in a matter of minutes. Feel free to add more veggies that you love like silverbeet, zucchini, asparagus or mushrooms, and serve with some paleo bread, if desired. It's also delicious teamed with smoked salmon or trout or fresh sardines.

BROCCOLI OMELETTE

200 g cherry tomatoes on the vine,
    snipped into 4 or 6 bunches
1 tablespoon olive oil
sea salt and freshly ground
    black pepper
80 ml (⅓ cup) melted coconut
    oil or good-quality animal fat*
½ onion, finely chopped
1 large head of broccoli (about 400 g),
    cut into small florets
2 garlic cloves, finely chopped
6 eggs
1 small handful of roughly chopped
    flat-leaf parsley leaves
Sauerkraut (page 322), to serve

* See Glossary

Preheat the oven to 180°C (160°C fan-forced). Line a baking tray with baking paper.

Place the cherry tomato bunches on the prepared tray, drizzle over the olive oil and sprinkle on some salt and pepper. Bake for 12 minutes, or until the tomatoes are softened and the skins start to blister.

Meanwhile, heat 1½ tablespoons of coconut oil or fat in a frying pan over medium heat. Add the onion and cook, stirring occasionally, for 5 minutes, or until softened and translucent. Add the broccoli and cook, tossing occasionally, for 2 minutes, or until just starting to colour. Pour in 125 ml (½ cup) of water and cook for 5 minutes, or until the water has evaporated and the broccoli is softened. Add 2 teaspoons of coconut oil or fat, stir in the garlic and cook for 1 minute. Season to taste with salt and pepper. Remove from the pan and keep warm.

Crack the eggs into a bowl and whisk lightly. Season with a pinch of salt and pepper.

Wipe the pan clean, add 1 tablespoon of the remaining oil or fat and heat over medium heat. Pour in half the egg mixture and tilt the pan so the mixture covers the base. Cook for 1 minute, or until the omelette is set underneath but still runny on top. Spoon half the cooked broccoli mixture onto one side of the omelette and cook for 1–2 minutes, or until the egg is lightly golden underneath and just set on top. Fold the uncovered half of the omelette over the broccoli, slide onto a serving plate and keep warm. Repeat this process to make a second omelette.

Scatter the parsley over the omelettes, divide the cherry tomatoes between the plates and serve with the sauerkraut on the side.

Serves 4

Shakshuka, a stand-out dish that originated in Israel, has taken the world by storm. We have put our personal spin on it and ramped it up with kale and silverbeet and an array of fresh herbs, to make the flavours sing. A touch of chilli takes this meal to the next level. Make a big batch and eat it straight from the pan. Any leftovers are a delicious inclusion in school or work lunch boxes the next day.

SILVERBEET AND KALE SHAKSHUKA

1 bunch of kale (about 300 g), stems discarded and leaves torn
1 bunch of silverbeet (about 800 g), stems removed and leaves torn (save the stems for stocks or broths)
25 g (½ packed cup) torn coriander leaves
70 g frozen peas, thawed
1 teaspoon chopped oregano leaves
250 ml (1 cup) Chicken or Beef Bone Broth (page 312 or 310) or vegetable stock, chilled
sea salt and freshly ground black pepper
2 tablespoons coconut oil or good-quality animal fat*
1 onion, chopped
4 garlic cloves, finely chopped
1 teaspoon ground cumin
1 teaspoon caraway seeds, ground in a spice grinder or using a mortar and pestle
4 eggs
1 handful of dill fronds
chilli oil, for drizzling

To serve (optional)
paleo bread, toasted
lemon wedges

* See Glossary

Blanch the kale and half the silverbeet in a large saucepan of boiling salted water for 30 seconds. Immediately transfer to a bowl of iced water and allow to cool. Drain and squeeze out the excess water.

Place the blanched greens in a high-speed blender, add the coriander, peas, oregano and broth or stock and blend until smooth. Season with salt and pepper.

Melt the oil or fat in a large frying pan over medium heat. Add the onion and cook for 5 minutes, or until softened and translucent. Stir in the garlic and spices and cook for 1 minute, or until fragrant. Add the remaining silverbeet, pop a lid on top and cook, stirring occasionally, for 3 minutes, or until wilted. Season with salt and pepper.

Pour the blended greens into the pan and stir through the sautéed onion and silverbeet. Using a spoon, create four small wells, then crack an egg into each well. Cover with a lid and gently simmer for 5–6 minutes, or until the egg whites are set but the yolks are still runny. Scatter over the dill and drizzle on the chilli oil. Serve with paleo toast and lemon wedges, if desired.

Tips
- You may like to serve your shakshuka with some dairy-free cashew, macadamia, pumpkin or zucchini 'cheese'. See the Snacks and Basics chapters for recipes.
- This dish is a great way to use up leftovers. Try adding some cooked seafood or sausage.

Serves 4

A lot of my recipes come about when I'm attempting to create something new and yummy for breakfast that also works for the kids' lunch boxes. I have found that fritters/hash browns/savoury pancakes fit the bill perfectly. This hash brown recipe uses the often-overlooked but delicious parsnip. I love the earthy nature of this underused vegetable and the way its sweetness works so well with zucchini to give it more body. I guarantee that once you make these you will be coming back for more.

PARSNIP AND ZUCCHINI HASH BROWNS

250 g grated zucchini
½ onion, thinly sliced
1 garlic clove, finely chopped
sea salt and freshly ground
    black pepper
400 g grated parsnip
2 teaspoons coconut flour
4 eggs
240 ml melted coconut oil
    or good-quality animal fat*

* See Glossary

Place the zucchini, onion and garlic in a colander, add 1 teaspoon of salt and mix well to combine. Stand for 15 minutes to allow the salt to draw out the excess liquid. Drain the liquid from the vegetables and, using your hands, squeeze out as much moisture as possible. Stir in the parsnip, coconut flour and eggs and season with salt and pepper.

Heat half the oil or fat in a large, deep non-stick frying pan over medium–high heat. Working in batches of three, spoon 2 tablespoons of veggie mixture per hash brown into the pan and flatten with a spatula to form a 1 cm thick rectangle or round. Cook for 2–3 minutes, or until golden and crisp, then flip over and cook on the other side until golden, crisp and cooked through. Drain on paper towel and cover to keep warm while frying the remainder, adding the remaining oil or fat as necessary. You should be left with 12 fritters. Season with a little salt and pepper, if desired, and serve immediately.

Tip
– The leftover oil or fat can be strained and reused as cooking oil for other recipes.

Serves 4

Also known as okonomiyaki, these ever-delightful Japanese cabbage pancakes will have the most hardened cabbage hater lining up for more. These pancakes are so moreish, they defy logic. I believe the charred cabbage, mayonnaise and seaweed makes for a perfect flavour combination. You can add seafood or bacon if you feel like a bit of meat, or simply add some mushrooms or carrots to stay on the vegetarian train. My advice is to make a heap of these, as leftovers are perfect for school and work lunches.

JAPANESE PANCAKES

6 eggs
2 tablespoons coconut flour
1 teaspoon baking powder
1 tablespoon tamari or coconut aminos*
½ teaspoon toasted sesame oil
150 g green cabbage, finely
   shredded on a mandoline
2 spring onions, white and green
   parts separated, thinly sliced
sea salt and freshly ground
   black pepper
80 ml (⅓ cup) melted coconut oil
   or good-quality animal fat*

To serve
100 ml Teriyaki Sauce (page 323)
150 g Japanese Mayonnaise (page 319)
1 toasted nori sheet,* thinly sliced
1–1½ teaspoons shichimi
   togarashi,* or to taste
2 tablespoons bonito flakes*

* See Glossary

Whisk the eggs, coconut flour, baking powder, tamari or coconut aminos and sesame oil in a bowl until there are no lumps. Add the cabbage and the white part of the spring onion and mix well to combine. Season with a little salt and pepper.

Heat a large non-stick frying pan over medium heat and add 1 tablespoon of oil or fat. Ladle in a quarter of the batter – about 125 ml (½ cup) – and spread out gently with the back of a spoon until about 13 cm in diameter. Cook the pancake for 2 minutes, or until the top dries out slightly and the bottom starts to brown. Flip and cook for an additional 2 minutes. Repeat with the remaining oil and pancake batter to make four pancakes.

Top each pancake with a drizzle of teriyaki sauce and mayonnaise, then sprinkle on the green part of the spring onion, nori, togarashi and bonito flakes.

Serves 4

We make a broth most weeks at home using chicken, beef or fish bones. This broth then becomes the base of many family meals, like curries, braises and soups. Simmering bones brings out nutritional powerhouses such as gelatine, collagen, glucosamine and calcium that our bodies love. For a quick breakfast, we simply add some veggies to whatever broth we have in the fridge and within 15 minutes we have a perfect meal. You could also add some chicken or fish for extra protein.

PUMPKIN AND SILVERBEET BROTH WITH CAULIFLOWER RICE

¼ small kent pumpkin (about 1 kg),
    cut into 8 wedges about 2 cm thick,
    peeled or unpeeled
3 tablespoons coconut oil or good-
    quality animal fat*, melted
sea salt and freshly ground
    black pepper
1 onion, chopped
4 silverbeet leaves, leaves torn
    and stems thinly sliced
2 garlic cloves, finely chopped
1½ teaspoons ground cumin
½ teaspoon ground coriander
1 teaspoon chopped thyme
1.25 litres Chicken Bone Broth
    (page 312) or vegetable stock
200 g uncooked Cauliflower Rice
    (page 312)
1 tablespoon lemon juice, or to taste
2 tablespoons finely chopped
    flat-leaf parsley leaves
2 tablespoons pumpkin seeds
    (activated if possible*)
½ lemon, peeled, zest cut into
    thin strips

* See Glossary

Preheat the oven to 220°C (200°C fan-forced).

Place the pumpkin wedges on a baking tray and drizzle with 1 tablespoon of oil or fat. Season with salt and pepper and roast for 30–35 minutes, or until tender and caramelised.

Meanwhile, heat the remaining oil or fat in a large saucepan over medium heat. Add the onion and silverbeet stems and cook, stirring occasionally, for 5–6 minutes, or until softened. Next, add the garlic, spices and thyme and cook for 20 seconds, or until fragrant. Pour in the broth or stock, bring to the boil, then reduce the heat to low and simmer for 20 minutes, or until the vegetables are softened and the flavours have developed.

Add the cauliflower rice and silverbeet leaves to the broth and simmer for a further 5 minutes, or until the silverbeet is wilted and the cauliflower rice is cooked through. Stir in the lemon juice and season to taste.

Divide the roasted pumpkin among four warm serving bowls and ladle in the hot broth and vegetables. Scatter over the parsley and pumpkin seeds and finish with the lemon zest.

Serves 4–6

If you don't have a spiraliser or a peeler that makes ribbons from your vegetables, then I have to say you are missing out. Only kidding! But, hey, it is a lot of fun to make vegetable noodles and use them to add flavour and nutrients to salads, soups and sauces. The great thing is the kids love them too. So, here is a recipe for veggie noodle pikelets that everyone will enjoy. Serve with the hollandaise below or any sauce or dip of your choice.

ZOODLE AND VEG PIKELETS

500 g zucchini, spiralised into
    thin noodles
250 g sweet potato, spiralised into
    thin noodles
1 carrot, spiralised into thin noodles
sea salt and freshly ground
    black pepper
1 handful of flat-leaf or curly parsley
    leaves, chopped
1 handful of baby spinach leaves,
    chopped
4 eggs
55 g (½ cup) almond meal
1 teaspoon baking powder
80 ml (⅓ cup) melted coconut oil

Hollandaise sauce
125 ml (½ cup) melted coconut oil
4 egg yolks
2 tablespoons lemon juice
    or apple cider vinegar
2 teaspoons finely chopped flat-leaf
    or curly parsley leaves

Place the zucchini, sweet potato and carrot noodles in a colander. Sprinkle on 2 teaspoons of salt and mix well. Stand for 15 minutes to allow the salt to draw out the excess liquid.

Meanwhile, to make the hollandaise sauce, warm the coconut oil in a saucepan to 50°C. Combine the egg yolks and lemon juice or vinegar in a blender. With the blender on low, slowly pour in the coconut oil in a thin, steady stream. Season with ½ teaspoon of salt, then pulse a few times to thicken. Mix through the parsley and set aside in a warm place until ready to serve.

Use your hands to squeeze out the excess moisture from the vegetable noodles. Make sure you remove as much liquid as possible, otherwise the pikelets will be soggy.

Place the vegetable noodles in a large bowl. Add the parsley, spinach, eggs, almond meal, baking powder and a pinch of pepper and mix well.

Heat the coconut oil in a non-stick frying pan over medium heat. Form a spoonful of the vegetable mixture into a golf ball–sized shape, then add straight to the pan and flatten with a spatula. Repeat with the remaining mixture. Fry the pikelets in batches of six to eight for 2 minutes on each side, or until golden brown and cooked through. Drain on paper towel. Serve the pikelets warm with the hollandaise sauce on the side.

Salads

Super Raw Salad with Avocado and Tahini Dressing/ Sweet and Sour Broccoli with Black Tahini/ Baby Beetroot and Walnut Salad/ Avo Bowl with Beetroot Spirals/ Seaweed and Cucumber Salad/ Mixed Salad Leaves with Avocado and Radish/ Zucchini, Kale and Avocado Salad with Hazelnut Pesto/ Avocado, Beetroot, Carrot and Spinach Rainbow Slaw/ Greek-Style Broccoli Salad/ Crunchy Cabbage Salad with Macadamia Nuts/ Capsicum Salad/ Fennel, Cucumber and Baby Cos Salad/ Italian Cauliflower Salad/ Broccoli Slaw/ Celery and Dukkah Tabbouleh/ Cucumber Tzatziki/ Fennel and Mint Salad/ Radicchio with Dukkah, Blistered Grapes and Pickled Shallots/ Charred Eggplant with Pomegranate and Nut 'Cheese'/ Roasted Pumpkin Tabbouleh/ Japanese-Style Carrot, Daikon and Cucumber Salad/ Cucumber and Pomegranate Salad with Toasted Walnuts/ Baby Spinach Salad with Honey–Mustard Dressing/ Sugar Snap, Radish and Rocket Salad/ Orange, Fennel and Walnut Salad/ Watercress Salad with Egg, Parsley and Red Onion/ Roasted Mushrooms with Spinach, Garlic and Thyme/ Curried Cauliflower and Egg Salad in Cos Lettuce Cups/ Watercress Salad with Pistachios and Preserved Lemon/ Gado Gado with Satay Sauce

Serves 4–6

There really is nothing more satisfying on a hot day than tucking into a delicious raw salad. Always have the freshest vegetables on hand to slice, shave, grate, spiralise, chop or dice; and use organic, where possible. These are some of my favourite ingredients to go into a raw salad. I have used a tahini dressing but feel free to dress your salad with mayo or a vinaigrette if you prefer. Some cooked prawns or chicken would work beautifully with this, too.

SUPER RAW SALAD WITH AVOCADO AND TAHINI DRESSING

1 small fennel bulb, thinly sliced using a mandoline or sharp knife
150 g savoy cabbage, thinly shredded using a mandoline or sharp knife
150 g red cabbage, thinly shredded using a mandoline or sharp knife
3 radishes, thinly sliced using a mandoline or sharp knife
1 Lebanese cucumber, halved, deseeded and cut into matchsticks
1 carrot, cut into matchsticks
1 large handful of rocket leaves
1 small handful of dill fronds
1 small handful of mint leaves
1 small handful of chopped flat-leaf parsley leaves
extra-virgin olive oil, for drizzling

Avocado and tahini dressing
1½ avocados, halved, stone removed and peeled
½ garlic clove, chopped
2 teaspoons finely chopped basil leaves
1½ tablespoons tahini (unhulled or hulled)
pinch of ground cumin
2 tablespoons lemon juice, plus extra for drizzling
2 tablespoons olive oil
sea salt and freshly ground black pepper

To make the dressing, place the avocado, garlic, basil and tahini in the bowl of a food processor and process until smooth and creamy. Add the cumin, lemon juice and olive oil and continue to whiz until smooth. Season with salt and pepper.

Arrange all the prepped salad ingredients on a large platter or in a large salad bowl, spoon over the dressing and drizzle some extra-virgin olive oil over the top. Drizzle over a little more lemon juice, if desired, and serve immediately.

Serves 4

Black sesame seeds are a little more pungent and bitter than white sesame seeds, and black tahini is simply unhulled black sesame seeds made into a paste by crushing them down. To make this dish a star, I have teamed this wonderful ingredient with a glorious broccoli salad that has texture, sweetness and some acidity.

SWEET AND SOUR BROCCOLI WITH BLACK TAHINI

80 ml (⅓ cup) extra-virgin olive oil
1½ tablespoons lemon juice
1½ tablespoons apple cider vinegar
1 tablespoon honey
1 teaspoon finely grated ginger
½ teaspoon sumac*
1 large head of broccoli (about 400 g), cut into florets, then thinly sliced
1 handful of almonds (activated if possible*), toasted and chopped
1 large handful of coriander leaves, torn
1 handful of mint leaves, torn
1 small handful of dill fronds
5 medjool dates, pitted and chopped
1–2 long red chillies, halved, deseeded and finely chopped (optional)
sea salt and freshly ground black pepper
2–3 tablespoons black tahini (see Note)

* See Glossary

In a large bowl, whisk together the olive oil, lemon juice, vinegar, honey and ginger until well combined. Add the sumac, broccoli, almonds, coriander, mint, dill, dates and chilli, if desired. Toss, then season with salt and pepper.

Smear the tahini over a platter or plates, top with the broccoli salad and serve.

Note
– You can buy black tahini at health-food stores and some supermarkets.
– Add some lamb, steak or seafood for extra protein.

Serves 4 as a side

Nut-based 'cheeses' have become super popular over the last few years. In this dish, I use cashew 'cheese' and team it with some roasted beetroot, which adds a lovely earthiness. Feel free to add salad leaves like rocket, radicchio or cos lettuce. You could also try other nuts or seeds to create your 'cheese' – macadamias work well.

BABY BEETROOT AND WALNUT SALAD

2 bunches of baby beetroot (about 20 beetroot), scrubbed, trimmed and halved (or quartered if large)
1 tablespoon coconut oil, melted
80 ml (⅓ cup) extra-virgin olive oil
2 tablespoons red wine vinegar or apple cider vinegar
2 teaspoons lemon juice
100 g (1 cup) walnut halves (activated if possible*), toasted and roughly chopped
sea salt and freshly ground black pepper
200 g (1 cup) Cashew 'Cheese' (page 311)
1 small handful of chives, cut into 5 cm lengths
1 handful of red-veined sorrel leaves
80 g (½ cup firmly packed) dried cherries, roughly chopped

* See Glossary

Preheat the oven to 200°C (180°C fan-forced).

Place the beetroot in a baking tray, then toss with the coconut oil to lightly coat. Cover tightly with baking paper or a lid and roast for 45–50 minutes, or until tender. When the beetroot are cool enough to handle, peel off their skins.

Combine the olive oil, vinegar, lemon juice and half the walnuts in a screw-top jar, season with a little salt and pepper and shake well.

Thickly spread the nut 'cheese' on plates or a large platter and top with the warm beetroot. Drizzle over some dressing, then scatter on the chives, sorrel and dried cherries. Season with salt and pepper. Finish with the remaining walnuts. Serve warm with the remaining dressing to pass at the table.

Serves 2

When avocados are in season my family and I stock up, and between us eat one or two a day! Avocados truly are one of the healthiest fats to consume and popping them in a salad bowl is a perfect way to honour this amazing low-carb fruit. To help the avo shine, I have teamed it with some of my other all-time favourite plant foods, including sauerkraut for good gut health. If you feel like adding protein, smoked fish, grilled sardines, cooked prawns, roasted or poached chicken or some ham would be perfect.

AVO BOWL WITH BEETROOT SPIRALS

10 g dried wakame,* chopped
250 ml (1 cup) boiling water
sea salt
1 bunch of broccolini (about 200 g),
    trimmed and halved
70 g baby green beans, trimmed
4 shiitake mushrooms, halved
1 large beetroot, spiralised into
    thin noodles
50 g Sauerkraut (page 322)
1 small handful of alfalfa sprouts
1 avocado, halved, stone removed
    and peeled
3 tablespoons Mayonnaise (page 320)
1 spring onion, green part only, thinly
    sliced (reserve the white part
    for other recipes)
black and white sesame seeds,
    for sprinkling

Dressing
1 tablespoon lemon juice
½ teaspoon Dijon mustard
1 teaspoon toasted sesame oil
1 tablespoon tamari or coconut aminos*
3 tablespoons extra-virgin olive oil

* See Glossary

Rehydrate the wakame in the boiling water for 5 minutes; drain, then season with a little salt.

Place all the dressing ingredients in a bowl and mix to combine.

Blanch the broccolini in salted boiling water for 3 minutes, or until just tender but still slightly crunchy. Remove with a slotted spoon or tongs and plunge into iced water. Drain and set aside. Using the same boiling water, blanch the beans and mushrooms for 1 minute, or until just tender. Again, plunge into iced water, then drain and set aside. Lastly, blanch the beetroot noodles in the salted boiling water for 15 seconds; plunge into iced water, then drain.

To serve, divide the beetroot noodles between two serving bowls, then add neatly arranged little piles of broccolini, beans, wakame, mushrooms, sauerkraut and alfalfa sprouts. Place an avocado half in the centre, dollop a spoonful of mayonnaise into the cavity, then drizzle with a good amount of dressing. To finish, scatter on the spring onion and sesame seeds.

Serves 4

I believe seaweed will become a prized form of nutrition as it can be harvested straight from the ocean, is super sustainable and damn delicious. Making your own seaweed salad is easy. Simply get some good-quality seaweed, either fresh or dried, then add a yummy dressing and some avocado, radish and cucumber. And why not include raw fish, roast chicken, cooked prawns or smoked trout, too?

SEAWEED AND CUCUMBER SALAD

30 g dried wakame,* chopped
500 ml (2 cups) boiling water
2 teaspoons toasted sesame oil
sea salt
3 Lebanese cucumbers, deseeded
   and cut into matchsticks
2 avocados, cut into 1 cm dice
4 radishes, cut into matchsticks
2 teaspoons white sesame seeds,
   toasted
1 teaspoon black sesame seeds, toasted
1 handful of chives, snipped into batons

Pickled daikon (see Note)
2 ½ tablespoons apple cider vinegar
1 tablespoon honey
1 teaspoon tamari or coconut aminos*
sea salt
150 g daikon, cut into matchsticks

Tamari and ginger dressing
2 tablespoons tamari or
   coconut aminos*
2 teaspoons finely grated ginger
1 tablespoon yuzu juice* or lemon juice
½ teaspoon chilli oil
2 tablespoons olive oil

To serve
80 g Mayonnaise (page 320)
1 teaspoon tamari or coconut aminos*

* See Glossary

You'll need to begin this recipe a day ahead if you want to pickle the daikon.

For the pickled daikon, bring the vinegar, honey, tamari or coconut aminos, 75 ml of water and a pinch of salt to the boil in a small saucepan. Add the daikon, set aside to cool, then cover and refrigerate overnight. Drain before use.

The next day, rehydrate the wakame in the boiling water for 5 minutes, then drain, then season with the sesame oil and a little salt and mix to combine.

Meanwhile, place all the tamari and ginger dressing ingredients in a bowl and mix well.

Arrange the wakame, cucumber, pickled daikon, avocado and radish on plates or a serving platter, drizzle over the dressing and sprinkle on the sesame seeds and chives. Spoon the mayonnaise into a small dish, drizzle with the tamari or coconut aminos and serve on the side.

Note
– Daikon can be eaten fresh, so if you don't have time to pickle it, just slice it up and enjoy.

Serves 2–4 as a side

The secret to a good salad is often the dressing, and one of the simplest and most delicious is the classic seeded mustard vinaigrette. This dressing elevates simple leaves to the most extravagant salad. I like to use sorrel leaves for this recipe as we grow them in our garden at home, but feel free to replace them with any type of lettuce or green of your choice. Try serving with sashimi, grilled sardines, roast chicken or pork.

MIXED SALAD LEAVES WITH AVOCADO AND RADISH

2 large handfuls of mixed salad leaves
1 small handful of baby sorrel leaves
   (if unavailable use another small
   handful of mixed salad leaves)
4–5 radishes, thinly sliced
1 avocado, sliced

Seeded mustard dressing
1 tablespoon seeded mustard
1 tablespoon lemon juice or
   apple cider vinegar
1 teaspoon honey
½ teaspoon finely grated ginger
3 tablespoons extra-virgin olive oil
sea salt and freshly ground
   black pepper

To make the dressing, place the mustard, lemon juice or vinegar, honey and ginger in a small bowl and whisk together. Slowly whisk in the olive oil until well combined. Season with salt and pepper.

To assemble the salad, place the salad leaves, sorrel (if using), radish and avocado in a large bowl or on a platter. Drizzle on the dressing and gently toss to coat. Season with some salt and pepper if needed.

Serves 4

Kale and zucchini are a match made in salad heaven. To take this pairing to the next level, add some good fats in the form of avocado and this amazing hazelnut pesto (it's so good you'll want to make extra and give it to your neighbours). Toss through some flaked smoked trout or halved boiled eggs or serve alongside roast chook or pork belly for a more substantial meal.

ZUCCHINI, KALE AND AVOCADO SALAD WITH HAZELNUT PESTO

½ bunch of curly kale (about 150 g),
    central stems discarded, leaves
    roughly chopped
1 tablespoon olive oil
3 zucchini, ends trimmed
1 avocado, sliced

Hazelnut pesto
2 garlic cloves, finely chopped
1 handful of basil leaves
1 handful of flat-leaf parsley leaves
70 g (½ cup) hazelnuts, toasted
    and chopped
200 ml extra-virgin olive oil
3 tablespoons lemon juice
2 teaspoons salted baby capers,
    rinsed well and patted dry
sea salt and freshly ground
    black pepper

Place the kale in a large bowl and pour over the olive oil. Rub the oil into the kale with your hands. (This removes the waxy coating on the kale and allows the leaves to absorb the dressing.) Set aside.

Next, using a mandoline or vegetable peeler, thinly slice the zucchini into long thick strips, then place in the bowl with the kale.

Combine all the hazelnut pesto ingredients in a small bowl.

When ready to serve, gently toss the zucchini and kale with the pesto and avocado. Arrange on plates or a large platter and serve.

Serves 2–4 as a side

My dear friend Dr Terry Wahls is a fan of eating rainbow slaw due to its high nutrient content. She attributes her recovery from multiple sclerosis to cutting out inflammatory foods (such as grains, legumes and dairy) and eating a diet high in vegetables (9 cups a day!) with a small amount of well-sourced nose-to-tail animal protein and fat. Here is a rainbow slaw to celebrate all the great work Terry is doing to help people reclaim their health.

AVOCADO, BEETROOT, CARROT AND SPINACH RAINBOW SLAW

1 avocado, cut into 1 cm dice
1 large beetroot, grated
1 large carrot, grated
2 large handfuls of baby spinach leaves
1 handful of chopped mint
1 handful of chopped flat-leaf
    parsley leaves
50 g (⅓ cup) pumpkin and sunflower
    seeds (activated if possible*), toasted

Dressing
1 tablespoon red wine vinegar
1 tablespoon lemon juice
½ French shallot, finely chopped
3 tablespoons extra-virgin olive oil
1 teaspoon honey
½ teaspoon Dijon mustard
sea salt and freshly ground
    black pepper

* See Glossary

Place all the dressing ingredients in a small bowl and whisk to combine.

Place all the salad ingredients in a serving bowl. Just before serving, pour the dressing over the salad and lightly toss.

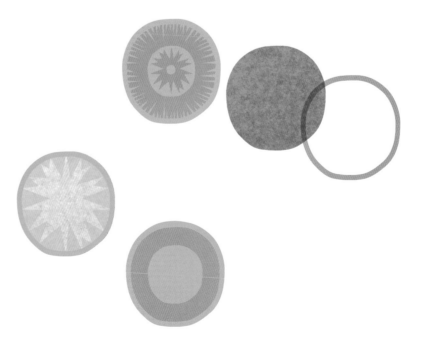

I am a huge lover of Greek food: roast lamb, avgolemono, tzatziki, amazing seafood and, of course, sensational vegetable and salad dishes. In this recipe I've given the classic Greek salad a nutritional makeover and replaced the feta with broccoli. If you want, add a side of seafood or roast lamb or goat.

GREEK-STYLE BROCCOLI SALAD

sea salt and freshly ground
    black pepper
1 large head of broccoli (about 400 g),
    cut into bite-sized florets
120 g Semi-Dried Tomatoes (page 322)
100 g pitted kalamata olives, halved
2 tablespoons sliced almonds, toasted
1 large handful of basil leaves

Pickled red onion
½ red onion, cut into 8 wedges
80 ml (⅓ cup) red wine vinegar
1 teaspoon honey

Dressing
100 ml extra-virgin olive oil
1 tablespoon lemon juice
1 garlic clove, finely grated
½ teaspoon Dijon mustard
1 teaspoon dried oregano

Place the pickled red onion ingredients in a small saucepan and bring to a simmer over medium heat. Cover with a lid and cook for 1 minute, then remove from the heat and allow to cool completely. Drain, reserving 2 tablespoons of the pickling vinegar for the dressing (save the rest for another use).

Combine all the dressing ingredients in a bowl and season to taste with salt and pepper. Add the reserved pickling vinegar and mix well.

Place the broccoli in a large bowl, pour over half the dressing and toss until the broccoli is well coated. Set aside to marinate for 30 minutes to allow the broccoli to soften slightly and become more flavoursome.

Add the pickled red onion, semi-dried tomatoes, olives, almonds and basil to the marinated broccoli and gently toss. Season with salt and pepper if needed. Arrange on a large platter, drizzle over some more dressing and serve.

Serves 2–4

Nothing says summer quite like the first mangoes of the season ripening on the trees and arriving at the markets. I adore using mangoes in desserts and warm-weather salads like this. To make this a more substantial meal, add cooked and chilled prawns, cold roast chicken or pork belly.

CRUNCHY CABBAGE SALAD WITH MACADAMIA NUTS

¼ Chinese cabbage (wombok) (about 300 g), thinly sliced
1 Lebanese cucumber, cut into long strips
1 green apple, cut into strips
½ mango, thinly sliced
2 spring onions, sliced on an angle
1–2 long red chillies, thinly sliced (optional)
2 handfuls of coriander leaves
75 g (½ cup) macadamia nuts (activated if possible*), toasted and chopped
sea salt and freshly ground black pepper

Dressing
3 tablespoons apple cider vinegar
80 ml (⅓ cup) extra-virgin olive oil
1 tablespoon tamari or coconut aminos*
1 teaspoon toasted sesame oil

* See Glossary

Combine all the dressing ingredients in a bowl and mix well.

To make the salad, arrange the cabbage, cucumber, apple and mango on a large platter. Scatter over the spring onion, chilli (if using), coriander leaves and macadamias, then drizzle on just enough dressing to coat. Season with salt and pepper.

Tip
– Any leftover dressing can be stored in a sealed jar in the fridge for up to 2 weeks.

Serves 4–6 as a side

Sometimes all you need are some colourful vegetables, a lovely dressing and, of course, a sharp knife. This is one of those salads that can be thrown together in a matter of minutes and is wonderful alongside a delicious roast or some barbecued meat or seafood. For a more luxurious salad, you may like to roast the capsicums and remove their skin.

CAPSICUM SALAD

3 red capsicums, cut into 5 mm strips
3 yellow capsicums, cut into
   5 mm strips
1 small red onion, thinly sliced into rings
100 ml sherry vinegar or
   apple cider vinegar
sea salt and freshly ground
   black pepper
80 ml (⅓ cup) extra-virgin olive oil
1 teaspoon dried oregano
1 large handful of basil leaves
1 handful of flat-leaf parsley leaves

Toss the capsicum, onion and vinegar in a large bowl and season with salt and pepper. Allow to sit for 15 minutes, or until the capsicum is slightly softened.

Just before serving, add the olive oil, dried oregano and fresh herbs and gently mix through.

Arrange the dressed salad on a platter, finish with a generous grinding of black pepper and serve.

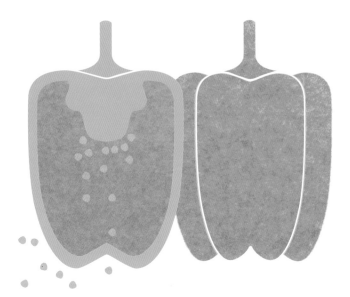

Serves 2–4 as a side

A simple salad of lettuce, cucumber and fennel is the perfect accompaniment to a home-cooked dinner. Try this with grilled or steamed fish, a roast or a barbecue of juicy snags or rib-eye steak.

FENNEL, CUCUMBER AND BABY COS SALAD

2 Lebanese cucumbers
1 large fennel bulb, trimmed and
    thinly shaved with a mandoline
    or sharp knife
2 baby cos lettuces, leaves separated
    and roughly torn
1 small handful of dill fronds
1 small handful of basil leaves
1 small handful of flat-leaf
    parsley leaves
sea salt and freshly ground
    black pepper

Lemon and mustard dressing
finely grated zest and juice of 1 lemon
1 teaspoon Dijon mustard
3 tablespoons extra-virgin olive oil

Using a vegetable peeler, shave the cucumbers lengthways into long strips, trying not to include any seeds. Discard the seeds.

Place the cucumber strips and fennel in a large bowl, then add the cos leaves, dill, basil and parsley. Set aside while you prepare the dressing.

To make the dressing, whisk together the lemon zest and juice, mustard and olive oil in a small bowl and season with salt.

Pour half the lemon and mustard dressing over the salad, then gently toss to combine. Season with pepper and a little extra salt if needed.

Arrange the salad on a large serving platter, then drizzle over the remaining dressing, if desired.

Serves 4 as a side

I adore this salad as it includes some of my all-time favourite ingredients that make Italian cooking so much fun: olives, capers, basil and chilli. When these are added to vegetables such as asparagus, mushrooms, roasted pumpkin or sweet potato, brussels sprouts, green beans, broccoli or, in this case, cauliflower you have a knock-out salad that works wonders with a perfect steak, roast chicken or grilled fish.

ITALIAN CAULIFLOWER SALAD

1 head of cauliflower (about 1 kg),
    cut into bite-sized florets
3 tablespoons coconut oil or
    good-quality animal fat,* melted
sea salt and freshly ground
    black pepper
5 garlic cloves, finely chopped
1 long red chilli, halved, deseeded
    and finely chopped (keep the seeds
    in if you like it spicy)
40 g salted baby capers, rinsed well
    and patted dry
90 g pitted kalamata olives, halved
1 tablespoon chopped flat-leaf
    parsley leaves
1 handful of oregano leaves,
    roughly chopped
2½ tablespoons red wine vinegar
    or lemon juice
80 ml (⅓ cup) extra-virgin olive oil
1 handful of basil leaves

* See Glossary

Preheat the oven to 200°C (180°C fan-forced). Line a baking tray with baking paper.

Blanch the cauliflower in boiling water for 2 minutes, or until just tender but still slightly crunchy in the centre. Drain and set aside to steam dry. (You don't want any moisture left on the cauliflower as it won't roast properly.) Drizzle 1 tablespoon of coconut oil or fat over the cauliflower and toss to coat. Scatter the cauliflower in a single layer over the prepared tray and season with salt and pepper. Roast for 15–20 minutes, or until the cauliflower is golden and tender.

Meanwhile, heat the remaining coconut oil or fat in a frying pan over medium heat, add the garlic and chilli and cook for about 30 seconds, or until they start to colour and become fragrant. Add the capers and olives and sauté for 1 minute. Remove the pan from the heat, add the parsley, oregano, vinegar or lemon juice and olive oil and toss through the caper and garlic mixture. Season with salt and pepper.

Place the cauliflower in a bowl, add the caper and garlic dressing and toss to evenly coat. Arrange the salad on a platter, scatter over the basil and serve warm or cold.

Why not take your slaw to the next level and add broccoli? Broccoli – a true wonder of the vegetable world – is the one vegetable I buy every week for the family as it is so very versatile and the kids love it. We use it in everything from soups, curries, roasts, salads and omelettes to replacing rice in nori rolls! Here you can elevate your slaw by adding raw or, if you prefer, lightly cooked and chilled broccoli. This slaw is perfect served with cooked prawns, smoked trout or topped with some shredded chicken.

BROCCOLI SLAW

sea salt and freshly ground
black pepper
1 large head of broccoli (about 400 g),
cut into bite-sized florets,
stems cut into matchsticks
200 g green cabbage, thinly shredded
1 green apple, cut into matchsticks
2 radishes, cut into matchsticks
2 spring onions, thinly sliced
1 handful of flat-leaf parsley leaves, torn
1 handful of mint leaves, torn
60 g almonds (activated if possible*),
toasted and chopped

Dressing
100 g Aioli (page 310) or
Mayonnaise (page 320)
1 tablespoon lemon juice
1 teaspoon filtered water

* See Glossary

To make the dressing, whisk together the aioli or mayonnaise, lemon juice and water in a small bowl. Season with salt and pepper. Set aside.

To make the slaw, combine all the ingredients in a large bowl, add half the dressing and toss gently. Drizzle over a little more dressing if required. Check the seasoning and add more salt and pepper if needed.

Tip
– Any leftover dressing can be stored in a sealed jar in the fridge for up to 2 weeks.

Serves 4 as a side

Of all the vegetables in the world celery is one of the most used, yet is rarely the star. It is often the backbone to many dishes, and in European cookery is used with onion and carrot as a flavour enhancer to form the base of stocks, braises and sauces. In its raw form it is included in many school lunch boxes. I want to show off celery's amazing taste and texture with this dish, which is inspired by the much-loved Middle Eastern tabbouleh. Serve alongside some grilled fish or seafood.

CELERY AND DUKKAH TABBOULEH

6 celery stalks, cut into small dice
1 handful of pale celery leaves
 (avoid the deeper green leaves
 as they tend to be bitter),
 finely chopped
2 spring onions, finely chopped
1 large handful of flat-leaf parsley
 leaves, finely chopped
3 tablespoons dukkah
80 g walnuts (activated if possible*),
 toasted and chopped
½ teaspoon sumac*
finely grated zest of 1 lemon
3 tablespoons lemon juice
3 tablespoons extra-virgin olive oil
sea salt and freshly ground
 black pepper
1–2 tablespoons chilli flakes (optional)

* See Glossary

Place the celery, celery leaves, spring onion, parsley, dukkah and half the walnuts in a large bowl. Add the sumac, lemon zest and juice and olive oil and toss well. Season with salt and pepper.

Arrange the tabbouleh in a serving bowl and sprinkle over the remaining walnuts and the chilli flakes, if using.

Serves 4 as a side

I love reinterpreting classic dishes in a modern way. To make the most of summer's abundance of cucumbers, I am always searching for ways to use them up. In this spin on Greek tzatziki, cucumber is given the chance to shine. Some grilled prawns or barbecued wild-caught salmon or roast lamb would be great to accompany it.

CUCUMBER TZATZIKI

sea salt and freshly ground
    black pepper
200 g Coconut Yoghurt (page 314)
4 Lebanese cucumbers, halved
    lengthways, then cut into
    2 cm thick wedges
1 handful of dill fronds,
    roughly chopped or torn
1 handful of mint leaves,
    roughly chopped or torn

Dressing
3 tablespoons lemon juice
100 ml extra-virgin olive oil
1 garlic clove, finely grated

Combine the dressing ingredients in a small bowl, season with salt and pepper and whisk well.

Place the coconut yoghurt in a serving bowl, add 2 tablespoons of the dressing and mix well.

Arrange the cucumber on a platter, scatter over the herbs, then pour over half the remaining dressing and gently toss to coat. Sprinkle on some salt and pepper and drizzle over a little extra dressing, if desired. Serve with the coconut yoghurt mixture on the side.

Tip
– Any leftover dressing can be stored in a sealed jar in the fridge for up to 3 weeks.

Serves 4 as a side

As a chef, I strive to respect the integrity of the flavour of my star ingredient. That is why I love the simplicity of this fennel salad. At the end of the day this dish is really just a couple of herbs and a dressing that complement the aniseed flavour of the fennel. Try serving this with grilled seafood or roast pork or lamb.

FENNEL AND MINT SALAD

2 fennel bulbs, trimmed, 1 handful
   of fronds reserved
¼ red onion, finely diced
1 handful of finely chopped mint leaves
1 handful of finely chopped dill fronds
sea salt and freshly ground
   black pepper

Dressing
1½ teaspoons finely chopped
   preserved lemon rind or
   finely grated lemon zest
3 tablespoons lemon juice
1 teaspoon Dijon mustard
80 ml (⅓ cup) extra-virgin olive oil

Finely chop the reserved fennel fronds, then, using a mandoline or sharp knife, thinly shave the bulbs.

Place the shaved fennel, fennel fronds, red onion and herbs in a large bowl and set aside while you prepare the dressing.

Combine all the dressing ingredients in a small bowl, season with salt and pepper and whisk well.

Pour just enough dressing over the salad to coat, then gently toss. Check for seasoning and add more salt and pepper if needed.

Arrange the fennel salad on a large platter and drizzle over a little more dressing, if desired.

Tip
– Any leftover dressing can be stored in a sealed jar in the fridge for up to 2 weeks.

Serves 4–6 as a side

I am a huge fan of Middle Eastern flavours in my kitchen. I find the spice combinations to be so seductive that I turn to this cuisine as often as I can. This simple salad teams dukkah, the famous nut and spice mix, with bitter radicchio and sweet cooked grapes. It's wonderful eaten alongside roast pork, duck or chicken.

RADICCHIO WITH DUKKAH, BLISTERED GRAPES AND PICKLED SHALLOTS

3 French shallots, thinly sliced
   into rounds with a mandoline
   or sharp knife
3 tablespoons sherry vinegar
400 g seedless red grapes
3 tablespoons extra-virgin olive oil
1 tablespoon lemon juice
sea salt and freshly ground
   black pepper
1½ heads of radicchio, leaves
   separated and roughly torn
2 tablespoons dukkah
1 small handful of chives,
   finely snipped

Place the shallot slices in a bowl and pour over 2 tablespoons of vinegar. Set aside for 10 minutes to allow the shallot slices to pickle slightly. Drain, reserving the liquid for the dressing.

Meanwhile, bring 80 ml (⅓ cup) of water to the boil in a large frying pan over medium–high heat. Add the grapes and, using a spatula, press down and squash so some juice seeps out. Cook for 5 minutes, or until the juice reduces to a syrup.

Transfer the grapes and syrup to a bowl. Add the olive oil, lemon juice and reserved shallot liquid, season with salt and pepper and gently toss together.

To serve, toss the radicchio with the grape dressing, scatter over the pickled shallots and sprinkle on the dukkah and chives.

Note
– You can lightly grill or roast the radicchio to enhance the flavour.

Serves 4

Eggplants have a meaty quality that makes them filling and satisfying. This terrific Middle Eastern eggplant salad with pomegranate molasses deserves a place in everyone's home. Its unique sweet and tart flavour is wonderful alone or served with grilled meat, seafood and vegetable dishes. I have included macadamia 'cheese' here, but that is just an idea if you have some in the fridge. You could also add some tahini.

CHARRED EGGPLANT WITH POMEGRANATE AND NUT 'CHEESE'

2 eggplants, cut into 1 cm thick rounds
sea salt and freshly ground
  black pepper
3 tablespoons melted coconut oil
  or olive oil
3 tablespoons extra-virgin olive oil
3 tablespoons apple cider vinegar
1 garlic clove, finely grated
2 tablespoons pomegranate molasses
1 handful of mint leaves, torn
2 large handfuls of rocket leaves
120 g Macadamia 'Cheese'
  (page 320) or other nut 'cheese'
  (optional)
seeds from ½ pomegranate

Place the eggplant in a colander, sprinkle with 2 teaspoons of salt and gently toss to coat. Set aside for 15 minutes to allow the bitter juices to drain. Lightly rinse the eggplant under cold water, then pat dry with paper towel.

Heat a barbecue or chargrill pan to medium–high heat.

Brush the coconut or olive oil over the eggplant, sprinkle on some salt and pepper, then cook, turning occasionally, for 5–6 minutes, or until charred and tender. Transfer to a serving plate.

Whisk the extra-virgin olive oil with the vinegar, garlic and 1 teaspoon of pomegranate molasses in a bowl.

Scatter the mint and rocket over the eggplant, then drizzle on the dressing, dollop on the nut 'cheese' (if using) and sprinkle on the pomegranate seeds. Drizzle over the remaining pomegranate molasses and serve.

Serves 2–4 as a side

When creating salads for the family, I generally look at the vegetables I need to use up and think about how they will work together. Pumpkin is the hero ingredient in this tabbouleh but you can use pretty much any vegetable that works with tomatoes, fresh herbs and a zingy little dressing. Pair it with some roast lamb, grilled fish or barbecued sausages for a delicious, healthy meal.

ROASTED PUMPKIN TABBOULEH

900 g butternut pumpkin, cut into
   3 cm pieces
1 teaspoon ground cumin
2 tablespoons coconut oil or
   good-quality animal fat,* melted
sea salt and freshly ground
   black pepper
60 g (½ cup) finely chopped cauliflower
1 large tomato, finely chopped
2 large handfuls of finely chopped
   flat-leaf parsley leaves
1 handful of finely chopped mint leaves
2 spring onions, finely chopped
1 tablespoon pumpkin seeds
   (activated if possible*), finely
   chopped (add more if you like)
3 tablespoons lemon juice
3 tablespoons extra-virgin olive oil

* See Glossary

Preheat the oven to 200°C (180°C fan-forced). Line a large baking tray with baking paper.

Place the pumpkin in a bowl and add the cumin and coconut oil or fat. Season with salt and pepper and toss to coat.

Arrange the pumpkin mixture in a single layer on the prepared tray. Roast for 35–40 minutes, or until the pumpkin is golden and tender. Allow to cool before adding to the salad.

Meanwhile, place the cauliflower, tomato, parsley, mint, spring onion, pumpkin seeds, lemon juice and olive oil in a bowl and mix to combine. Season with a little salt and pepper. Add the cooled pumpkin, gently toss and serve.

Serves 4–6 as a side

Japanese cuisine has a wonderful affinity with clean eating. Walk into any sashimi restaurant and see how meticulous the kitchen is and then witness the Zen-like quality the chefs bring to slicing a fillet of fish. There is also great reverence for all types of vegetable in Japanese cooking. I love what they can do with staple ingredients like carrot and cucumber and how they elevate them with a delicious dressing. Serve this alongside grilled chicken skewers or a whole roasted fish.

JAPANESE-STYLE CARROT, DAIKON AND CUCUMBER SALAD

2 Lebanese cucumbers, halved, deseeded and cut into thin matchsticks
2 carrots, cut into matchsticks
⅓ daikon, cut into matchsticks
sea salt and freshly ground black pepper
1 large handful of bean sprouts, trimmed
1½ tablespoons toasted sesame seeds

Dressing
2½ tablespoons tamari or coconut aminos*
2½ tablespoons apple cider vinegar
½ teaspoon coconut sugar or honey
pinch of sea salt
¼ teaspoon mustard powder (optional)
1 tablespoon olive oil
1 tablespoon toasted sesame oil

* See Glossary

To make the dressing, combine all the ingredients with 1 tablespoon of water in a small bowl and whisk well.

Dress the cucumber, carrot and daikon with a little dressing and arrange in serving bowls or on a platter. Season with a little salt and pepper if needed. Spoon more of the dressing over the top, then scatter on the bean sprouts and sesame seeds.

Tip
– Any leftover dressing can be stored in a sealed jar in the fridge for up to 3 weeks.

Serves 4 as a side

I encourage you to get adventurous with nuts and seeds and try including them in salads for added texture and flavour. Start with the basics: look at including cashews with Asian dishes; pine nuts, walnuts and pistachios with Middle Eastern recipes; almonds and hazelnuts with European flavours; and macadamias, well, they go with everything. Try this salad paired with some smoked fish or roast chicken.

CUCUMBER AND POMEGRANATE SALAD WITH TOASTED WALNUTS

5 Lebanese cucumbers
seeds of ½ pomegranate
1 handful of mint leaves,
    roughly chopped
2 tablespoons snipped chives
1 small handful of chervil sprigs
100 g (1 cup) walnuts (activated if
    possible*), toasted and chopped
sea salt
1 tablespoon pomegranate molasses

Lemon dressing
juice of 1 lemon
3 tablespoons extra-virgin olive oil

* See Glossary

Using a vegetable peeler, shave the cucumbers lengthways into long strips, trying not to include any seeds. Discard the seeds.

Place the cucumber strips in a large bowl, then add the pomegranate seeds, mint, chives, chervil and walnuts. Set aside while you prepare the dressing.

To make the dressing, whisk the lemon juice and olive oil in a small bowl and season with salt.

Pour half the lemon dressing over the salad, then gently toss to combine. Season with a little extra salt if needed.

Arrange the salad on a large serving platter, then drizzle over the pomegranate molasses and the remaining dressing.

I made a version of this salad for years in my restaurants, as it was such a crowd pleaser. I still put it together for my family when I can get my hands on some organic baby spinach. At its simplest, all you need to add is a good flavoured dressing and some fresh herbs. You could also include a dollop or two of nut 'cheese' or dairy-free pesto or some sliced, grilled lamb.

BABY SPINACH SALAD WITH HONEY–MUSTARD DRESSING

sea salt and freshly ground
    black pepper
3 large handfuls of baby spinach leaves
2 handfuls of rocket leaves
1 red onion, thinly sliced with
    a mandoline or sharp knife
1 handful of flat-leaf parsley leaves, torn
1 handful of mint leaves, torn

Honey–mustard dressing
1 garlic clove, finely grated
3 tablespoons apple cider vinegar
1 tablespoon Dijon mustard
1 tablespoon honey
125 ml (½ cup) extra-virgin olive oil

To make the dressing, whisk the garlic, vinegar, mustard and honey together in a small bowl. Slowly whisk in the olive oil until the dressing is emulsified. Season with salt and pepper.

Combine the spinach, rocket, red onion and herbs in a bowl, pour over just enough dressing to coat, then gently toss. Season with salt and pepper and add more dressing, if desired. Serve immediately in a salad bowl or on a large platter.

Tip
– Any leftover dressing can be stored in a sealed jar in the fridge for up to 3 weeks.

A salad of sugar snap peas teamed with radish and rocket can enhance the family dining experience, from a taste as well as a nutritional point of view. We say that we eat with our eyes first and foremost, and you can't deny that this dish screams to be eaten. This salad is terrific alongside some roast chicken or grilled fish.

SUGAR SNAP, RADISH AND ROCKET SALAD

500 g sugar snap peas
1 tablespoon coconut oil
   or good-quality animal fat*
3 garlic cloves, chopped
sea salt and freshly ground
   black pepper
2 handfuls of baby rocket leaves
6 radishes, quartered
1 small handful of chervil sprigs
finely grated zest of ½ lemon

Dressing
juice of 1 lemon
2 teaspoons chopped flat-leaf
   or curly parsley leaves
3 tablespoons lemon-infused
   olive oil

* See Glossary

Remove and discard the stem end and string from the sugar snap peas.

Melt the oil or fat in a large frying pan over medium heat. Add the sugar snap peas, garlic and a pinch of salt and pepper and sauté, tossing occasionally, for 3–5 minutes, or until the sugar snap peas are tender crisp. Set aside to cool completely.

Place the sugar snaps peas in a large bowl, then add the rocket, radish and chervil. Set aside while you prepare the dressing.

To make the dressing, whisk together the lemon juice, parsley and olive oil in a small bowl and season to taste with salt.

Pour half the dressing over the salad, then gently toss to combine. Season with a little extra salt if needed.

Arrange the salad on a large serving platter, then drizzle over the remaining dressing, if desired, and sprinkle over the lemon zest.

Tip
– I have sautéed the sugar snaps here, but you can blanch them or leave them raw if you prefer.

Serves 4–6 as a side

A citrus-based salad using ripe orange and the bitter leaves of radicchio, witlof or dandelion is simply sensational. The addition of thinly sliced fennel, which brings in an aniseed flavour, some crunchy walnuts and an acidic dressing is all you need for a wonderful lunch. You could add some cooked and chilled prawns, roast chicken or grilled duck breast to make this a more substantial meal.

ORANGE, FENNEL AND WALNUT SALAD

1 large fennel bulb, trimmed and
  fronds reserved
1 large head of radicchio, leaves
  separated and roughly torn
2 oranges, flesh cut into segments
1 handful of dill fronds
1 handful of basil leaves
80 g walnuts (activated if possible*),
  toasted and roughly chopped
sea salt and freshly ground
  black pepper

Balsamic dressing
3 tablespoons balsamic vinegar
125 ml (½ cup) extra-virgin olive oil
1 teaspoon honey
1 teaspoon Dijon mustard

* See Glossary

Using a mandoline or sharp knife, thinly shave the fennel.

Place the shaved fennel, radicchio, orange segments, herbs, walnuts and fennel fronds in a large bowl and set aside while you prepare the dressing.

To make the dressing, place all the ingredients in a small bowl and whisk to combine. Season with salt and pepper.

Pour just enough dressing over the salad to coat, then gently toss. Check for seasoning and add more salt and pepper if needed.

Arrange the salad on a large platter and drizzle over a little more dressing, if desired.

Tip
– Any leftover dressing can be stored in a sealed jar in the fridge for up to 2 weeks.

Serves 2–4 as a side

Watercress is a potent and nutritious leafy green that I love to grow in my garden, as it has a lovely pepperiness that really gives a lift to dishes. Here, one of nature's other superfoods, the humble boiled egg, is combined with the watercress to create a wonderfully rich dish. You can serve this with any type of seafood (it loves grilled sardines) or, if you want to keep it vegetarian, some roasted beetroot.

WATERCRESS SALAD WITH EGG, PARSLEY AND RED ONION

sea salt and freshly ground
    black pepper
2 large handfuls of watercress sprigs,
    trimmed
2 large handfuls of flat-leaf
    parsley leaves
½ red onion, finely diced
3 tablespoons salted baby capers,
    rinsed well and patted dry
4 hard-boiled eggs, peeled
    and crumbled

Dressing
3 tablespoons red wine vinegar or
    apple cider vinegar
½ teaspoon honey
80 ml (⅓ cup) extra-virgin olive oil

Combine all the dressing ingredients in a small bowl and mix well. Season with salt and pepper.

Place the watercress, parsley, red onion, capers and egg in a large salad bowl, drizzle on just enough dressing to coat the leaves and lightly toss. Season with salt and pepper and drizzle over more dressing, if desired. Serve immediately.

Tip
– Any leftover dressing can be stored in a sealed jar in the fridge for up to 3 weeks.

Serves 4 as a side

Mushrooms can be used in so many dishes. They can be made into a sauce to serve on your roast chicken or grilled steak or they can be added to your stir-fries, soups, braises, curries and salads. They bring a lovely earthiness to your meals and, to me, scream of autumn and winter. Here is a wonderful side dish that you can serve with your poached eggs, snags or roast.

ROASTED MUSHROOMS WITH SPINACH, GARLIC AND THYME

800 g button mushrooms, cleaned
2 teaspoons finely chopped thyme
5 French shallots, quartered
2½ tablespoons coconut oil or
    good-quality animal fat,* melted
sea salt and freshly ground
    black pepper
4 garlic cloves, finely chopped
2 large handfuls of baby spinach leaves
finely grated zest of ½ lemon
2 tablespoons balsamic vinegar
3 tablespoons extra-virgin olive oil,
    plus extra to serve

* See Glossary

Preheat the oven to 180°C (160°C fan-forced).

Place the mushrooms, thyme and shallot in a large roasting tin, toss with 2 tablespoons of coconut oil or fat and season with salt and pepper. Spread out the mushrooms and shallot to form a single layer and roast for 25–30 minutes, or until the mushrooms and shallot are tender and golden.

Heat the remaining oil or fat in a large frying pan over medium heat. Add the garlic and cook for 30 seconds, or until fragrant. Remove from the heat.

Place the spinach, roasted mushrooms and shallot, lemon zest, balsamic, olive oil and garlic in a large bowl and give everything a good toss. Season with salt and pepper if needed and transfer to a platter. Drizzle over a little extra olive oil and serve.

Serves 4

The combination of good-quality curry power, homemade aioli or mayo and boiled eggs is unbeatable. I have upped the vegetable component by adding the ever-versatile cauliflower and wrapped it up in some lettuce cups for a fun meal or lunch-box addition. You could wrap your egg salad in nori seaweed or use witlof leaves instead of the cos. Try adding some smoked trout, cooked tuna, prawns or chicken for extra protein.

CURRIED CAULIFLOWER AND EGG SALAD IN COS LETTUCE CUPS

½ head of cauliflower (about 500 g), cut into small florets
1 tablespoon curry powder
1 tablespoon coconut oil or good-quality animal fat,* melted
sea salt and freshly ground black pepper
1 teaspoon Dijon mustard
120 g Aioli (page 310) or Mayonnaise (page 320)
4 hard-boiled eggs, peeled and chopped
2 tablespoons chopped flat-leaf parsley leaves
2 teaspoons olive oil, plus extra to serve
1 baby cos lettuce, trimmed and leaves separated
lemon wedges, to serve (optional)

* See Glossary

Preheat the oven to 180°C (160°C fan-forced). Line a baking tray with baking paper.

In a large bowl, combine the cauliflower, curry powder and oil or fat and toss until well coated. Season with salt and pepper and place in a single layer on the prepared tray. Roast for 17–20 minutes, stirring and tossing halfway through, until the cauliflower is golden but still slightly crunchy. Allow to cool.

Meanwhile, mix the mustard with the aioli or mayo in a small bowl.

Place the cauliflower, egg, parsley, olive oil and aioli or mayo in a large bowl and gently mix until the cauliflower and egg are well coated. Season with extra salt and pepper if needed.

Spoon the curried cauliflower and egg salad into the cos lettuce cups, drizzle with a little extra olive oil and squeeze over some lemon juice, if desired.

If you are going to serve a green salad, why not go the whole hog and make it the star of the meal? For me, this is one hell of a salad. It has watercress for freshness and pepperiness, avocado for luscious healthy fat, pistachios add their unique texture and flavour, and preserved lemon and fresh herbs provide a Middle Eastern zing. A grilled or steamed piece of salmon or a medium–rare steak served alongside are the perfect accompaniments.

WATERCRESS SALAD WITH PISTACHIOS AND PRESERVED LEMON

2 large handfuls of watercress
   sprigs, trimmed
1 handful of basil leaves
1 handful of dill fronds
50 g pistachio kernels, lightly
   toasted and roughly chopped
50 g preserved lemon, flesh chopped
   into 5 mm pieces, rind thinly sliced
1 avocado, cut into 1 cm dice
sea salt and freshly ground
   black pepper

Dressing
80 ml (⅓ cup) extra-virgin olive oil
1½ tablespoons lemon juice
   or apple cider vinegar

Place the watercress, herbs, pistachios, preserved lemon flesh and rind and avocado in a large bowl and set aside while you prepare the dressing.

Combine all the dressing ingredients in a small bowl, season with salt and pepper and whisk well.

Pour just enough dressing over the salad to coat, then gently toss. Check for seasoning and add salt and pepper if needed.

Arrange the watercress salad on a large platter and drizzle over a little more dressing, if desired.

Serves 4

On my first trip to Indonesia about 25 years ago I remember ordering the famous gado gado, a mixture of assorted vegetables topped with a delicious satay sauce. This version uses some of my all-time favourite ingredients while retaining the essence of the original salad I devoured in Bali all those years ago. Some grilled chicken satay sticks would work well with this, too.

GADO GADO WITH SATAY SAUCE

1 bunch of asparagus (about 8 spears), woody ends trimmed
2 baby bok choy, trimmed
1 turnip, cut into 2 cm pieces
½ Lebanese cucumber, sliced
1 large handful of bean sprouts, trimmed
6 fresh okra pods, halved lengthways
100 g Chinese cabbage (wombok), shredded
3 hard-boiled eggs, peeled and halved lengthways
1 handful of coriander leaves
1 long red chilli, sliced (optional)

Satay sauce
160 g (1 cup) macadamia nuts (activated if possible*)
120 g almond butter
2 tablespoons finely grated ginger
1 long red chilli, halved, deseeded and sliced
2 tablespoons tamari or coconut aminos*
1 tablespoon toasted sesame oil
1 tablespoon maple syrup
fish sauce or sea salt, to taste (optional)

* See Glossary

To make the satay sauce, combine the macadamias and almond butter in the bowl of a food processor and pulse until ground. Add the ginger and chilli and process to combine. Add the tamari or coconut aminos, sesame oil and maple syrup and whiz, then gradually pour in 100 ml of water and pulse until the sauce is smooth. If the sauce is a little too thick, simply add more water. Season with a little fish sauce or salt, if desired. Transfer the satay sauce to a saucepan over medium heat and stir constantly until heated through, adding a little more water if needed. Keep warm.

Blanch the asparagus, bok choy and turnip separately in boiling salted water until just tender. The asparagus and bok choy take about 1 minute and the turnip takes about 5 minutes. Refresh briefly in cold water, then drain.

Arrange the cooked vegetables on a large platter along with the cucumber, bean sprouts, okra, Chinese cabbage, eggs, coriander leaves and chilli (if using). Serve with a bowl of the satay sauce on the side to drizzle over the salad.

Note
– Any leftover satay sauce can be stored in an airtight container in the fridge for up to 2 weeks.

Global Flavours

Roasted Carrot and Pickled Radish with Green Tahini/ Bok Choy with Garlic, Ginger and Mushrooms/ Celery and Daikon with Ponzu/ Vietnamese Pickled Carrot, Cucumber and Daikon/ Asian Greens/ Cauliflower Pakora with Coriander and Mint Sauce/ Thai Roasted Pumpkin with Satay Sauce/ Palakoora Vepadu/ Roasted Cauliflower with Fish Sauce Dressing/ Miso-Glazed Bok Choy/ Kung Pao Cauliflower/ Asian Greens with Typhoon Garlic/ Roasted Brussels Sprouts with Miso/ Roasted Cauliflower Larb/ Celery Stir-Fry/ Steamed Broccolini and Spinach with Ginger–Miso Dressing/ Sautéed Daikon with Garlic/ Spinach and Walnut Pkhali/ Chinese-Style Steamed Eggplant/ Onion Bhajis with Minted Mayonnaise/ Charred Spring Onions with Ginger and Tamari/ Miso-Glazed Roasted Eggplant with Dashi/ Tomato-Braised Okra with Za'atar/ Thai Green Curry/ Mushroom Stir-Fry with Jalapeno Dressing/ Vegetable Masala

Serves 4–6 as a side

In the '70s, when I was growing up, honey carrots were a bit of a gourmet thing. Since then, the carrot has taken a back seat in the culinary world. I believe it needs to reclaim its spot at the top, as it truly is a delicious and versatile ingredient. For this recipe, I have teamed roasted carrot with a green tahini sauce and some pickled radish and dukkah to add a lovely crunch and some much-needed spice. Perfect served with grilled fish, roast lamb or chicken. This dish was inspired by chef Tom Walton, who makes vegetables shine like no one else!

ROASTED CARROT AND PICKLED RADISH WITH GREEN TAHINI

sea salt and freshly ground
    black pepper
4 large carrots, cut into 1 cm
    thick rounds
½ teaspoon ground cumin
2 tablespoons coconut oil or
    good-quality animal fat,* melted
12–15 pieces of Pickled Radish
    (page 320)
1 handful of dill fronds
2 tablespoons dukkah

Green tahini
3 tablespoons hulled tahini
80 g Coconut Yoghurt (page 314)
2 tablespoons lemon juice
2 tablespoons olive oil
2 large handfuls of curly or
    flat-leaf parsley leaves
1 handful of dill fronds
2 spring onions, sliced
2 garlic cloves, chopped

* See Glossary

Preheat the oven to 200°C (180°C fan-forced). Line a large baking tray with baking paper.

Place all the green tahini ingredients in a high-speed blender, add some salt and pepper and blend until smooth and creamy. The sauce should be slightly thick like a mayonnaise; add some water if needed.

Bring a large saucepan of water to the boil. Blanch the carrot for 5 minutes. Drain and allow to cool slightly.

Place the carrot in a bowl, add the cumin and oil or fat, season with salt and pepper and toss to coat. Arrange the carrot in a single layer on the prepared tray. Roast for 30 minutes, or until the carrot is golden and tender.

To serve, spoon the green tahini onto a platter and smear to cover the base. Arrange the roasted carrot and pickled radish on top, then sprinkle on the dill and dukkah.

Serves 4 as a side

I absolutely love bok choy teamed with a simple sauce or dressing that elevates it to new gastronomic heights. For this recipe, I have added some shiitake and oyster mushrooms to make it a little 'meatier'. This dish is wonderful with steamed salmon or poached chicken.

BOK CHOY WITH GARLIC, GINGER AND MUSHROOMS

4 baby bok choy, halved lengthways
sea salt and freshly ground
    black pepper
2 tablespoons coconut oil or
    good-quality animal fat*
5 garlic cloves, finely chopped
5 cm piece of ginger,
    cut into matchsticks
150 g shiitake mushrooms,
    roughly chopped
150 g oyster mushrooms, roughly torn
125 ml (½ cup) Chicken Bone
    Broth (page 312), vegetable
    stock or water
2 tablespoons tamari or
    coconut aminos*
1 teaspoon apple cider vinegar
2 teaspoons honey
1 teaspoon toasted sesame oil
1 handful of coriander sprigs

* See Glossary

Place the bok choy in a single layer in a steamer basket over a saucepan of boiling water. Cover and steam for about 5 minutes, or until the bok choy is tender. Season with salt and pepper.

Meanwhile, heat the oil or fat in a wok or large saucepan over medium–high heat until it starts to sizzle. Add the garlic and ginger and stir-fry for 15 seconds, or until fragrant. Next, add the shiitake and oyster mushrooms and stir-fry for 30 seconds. Reduce the heat to medium, pour in the broth, stock or water, the tamari or coconut aminos, vinegar, honey and sesame oil and toss through the mushrooms. Cook for 1½ minutes, then remove from the heat.

Pour the mushrooms and sauce into a serving dish, arrange the steamed bok choy on top and scatter over the coriander.

Serves 2–4 as a side

Celery and daikon are two often-overlooked ingredients that really deserve the limelight, not only for their taste but also for their nutritional properties. This is a simple recipe that enlivens the tastebuds and makes a great addition to grilled or steamed fish.

CELERY AND DAIKON WITH PONZU

1 tablespoon coconut oil or good-quality animal fat*
6 celery stalks, cut into matchsticks
¼ daikon, cut into matchsticks
1 tablespoon Furikake Seasoning (page 318), plus extra if desired
1 small handful of radish sprouts, baby shiso leaves or micro herb of your choice, to serve

Ponzu
2 tablespoons tamari or coconut aminos*
2 teaspoons lemon juice
½ teaspoon finely grated ginger
1 garlic clove, finely grated
½ teaspoon toasted sesame oil
3 tablespoons bonito flakes*

* See Glossary

To make the ponzu, mix all the ingredients with 3 tablespoons of water in a small bowl. Allow to stand at room temperature for 30 minutes for the flavours to infuse. Strain the ponzu mixture through a fine sieve into a bowl and squeeze out as much liquid as possible from the bonito, then discard the bonito.

Heat the oil or fat in a wok or large frying pan over medium–high heat. Add the celery and sauté for 3 minutes, or until still slightly crisp in the centre.

Place the sautéed celery on a serving platter, pour over the ponzu, then top with the daikon and furikake seasoning. Mix it all up with some chopsticks or tongs, add some more furikake seasoning if needed. Top with the micro herbs, then serve.

Makes 1 × 1 litre jar

Pickled veggies are taking the world by storm again. I have to say this Vietnamese-style vegetable pickle is one of my favourites. The combination of carrot, daikon and cucumber makes for the most sublime profile of textures and flavours. It works so well alongside fresh Asian herbs, lettuce, cabbage leaves and all manner of grilled seafood, meat and delicious Vietnamese pancakes.

VIETNAMESE PICKLED CARROT, CUCUMBER AND DAIKON

150 ml filtered water
180 ml apple cider vinegar
1 tablespoon honey
1¼ teaspoons sea salt
1½ tablespoons fish sauce
200 g carrot (about 2),
    cut into matchsticks
125 g daikon (about ¼),
    cut into matchsticks
3 Lebanese cucumbers,
    halved lengthways,
    deseeded and cut
    into matchsticks
3 garlic cloves, finely chopped
½ teaspoon finely grated ginger
1½ tablespoons finely chopped
    coriander stalks and roots
1 long red chilli, halved lengthways

You will need a 1 litre glass jar with an airtight lid for this recipe. Wash the jar and all the utensils you will be using in very hot water or run them through a hot rinse cycle in the dishwasher.

Combine the water, vinegar, honey, salt and fish sauce in a large bowl and mix until well combined.

In another bowl, combine the carrot, daikon, cucumber, garlic, ginger, coriander and chilli, then gently mix.

Fill the prepared jar with the vegetable mixture, then pour in the pickling liquid. The vegetables should be completely submerged in the liquid. Cover with the lid and place in the fridge for at least 2 days. For best results, and to allow the veggies to become more flavourful and tangy, pickle for 3–4 days. Once opened, the pickled veggies submerged in the liquid will keep for up to 3 weeks in the fridge.

Serves 4 as a side

One of the things I really love about eating in Asian restaurants is that they serve some of the best vegetable sides. Whether it be sambal okra from Malaysia, morning glory from Singapore, wok-tossed Chinese broccoli with oyster sauce from China or this simple spinach and sesame number, these types of greens make the perfect accompaniment to roasted meat or steamed fish.

ASIAN GREENS

2 tablespoons coconut oil or
    good-quality animal fat*
4 garlic cloves, finely chopped
6 dried long red chillies (optional)
3 bunches of English spinach,
    trimmed and roughly chopped
sea salt and freshly ground
    black pepper
2 teaspoons sesame seeds,
    toasted, to serve

Tamari sauce
2 tablespoons tamari or
    coconut aminos*
2½ tablespoons Chicken Bone
    Broth (page 312) or water
1 teaspoon toasted sesame oil

* See Glossary

Place all the tamari sauce ingredients in a small saucepan and bring to a simmer over medium heat. Remove from the heat and keep warm.

Melt the oil or fat in a large non-stick frying pan over medium–high heat. Add the garlic and dried chillies (if using) and stir-fry for 20 seconds, or until fragrant. Add the spinach, in batches, and cook for 2–2½ minutes, or until the spinach is just wilted. Season with salt and pepper.

Transfer the spinach to a large serving platter and pour over a little of the sauce. Scatter the sesame seeds over the top and serve with the remaining sauce on the side.

Serves 4

I adore vegetable fritters that can be served as a snack, a school or work lunch or alongside a delicious meal as part of a banquet. Here, I have used lightly spiced cauliflower for the fritters – or pakora – and served them with a tantalising coriander and mint sauce that takes these little morsels to the next level.

CAULIFLOWER PAKORA WITH CORIANDER AND MINT SAUCE

sea salt and freshly ground
    black pepper
100 g cooked Cauliflower Rice
    (page 312), chilled
1 leek, white part only,
    finely chopped
1 long red chilli, thinly sliced
2 garlic cloves, finely chopped
1 teaspoon ground coriander
2 tablespoons almond meal
1 tablespoon coconut flour
4 eggs, beaten
coconut oil, for deep-frying

Coriander and mint sauce
1 large handful of coriander leaves
1 handful of mint leaves
2 long green chillies, halved,
    deseeded and roughly chopped
1 garlic clove, roughly chopped
½ teaspoon ground cumin
1½ tablespoons apple cider vinegar
200 g Mayonnaise (page 320)

For the coriander and mint sauce, place the coriander, mint, chilli, garlic and cumin in the bowl of a food processor and process until finely chopped. Add the vinegar and process until smooth. Pour the mixture into a bowl, then stir in the mayonnaise. Season to taste with salt and pepper and refrigerate until needed.

Combine the cauliflower rice with the leek, chilli, garlic and ground coriander in a bowl. Add the almond meal, coconut flour and egg and mix to form a thick doughy batter. Season with salt and pepper.

Melt the oil in a large saucepan over medium–high heat until the temperature reaches about 160°C. (To test, drop a teaspoon of batter into the hot oil; if it starts bubbling straight away, it is ready.) Using a soup spoon, shape the batter into balls and carefully lower them into the hot oil in batches of six to eight. Deep-fry, turning occasionally, for about 2 minutes, or until the pakora are golden brown and cooked through. Drain on paper towel. You should get about 20 pakora. Serve hot with the coriander and mint sauce for dipping.

Serves 4 as a side

Roasted pumpkin features on the menu at home every week or so, and, really, you don't have to do too much to make it shine. Whether it be a light dusting of cumin, some rosemary and garlic, a salsa verde or perhaps a spiced chilli sauce, once the pumpkin comes out of the oven, you are pretty much guaranteed a hit on the plate. This is one of my favourite ways to serve it. Try it alongside some grilled chicken, roast pork or seared salmon.

THAI ROASTED PUMPKIN WITH SATAY SAUCE

½ kent pumpkin, cut into
    4 cm wedges
2 tablespoons coconut oil or
    good-quality animal fat,* melted
fish sauce or sea salt, to taste
juice of ½ lime
60 g pumpkin seeds (activated
    if possible*), toasted
1 long red chilli, thinly sliced
12 green peppercorn stalks in
    brine (optional)
1 handful of coriander leaves
1 large handful of Thai basil leaves

Satay sauce
160 g (1 cup) macadamia nuts
    (activated if possible*)
120 g almond butter
2 tablespoons finely grated ginger
1 long red chilli, halved, deseeded
    and sliced
2 tablespoons tamari or
    coconut aminos*
1 tablespoon toasted sesame oil
1 tablespoon maple syrup
fish sauce or sea salt, to taste (optional)

* See Glossary

Preheat the oven to 200°C (180°C fan-forced).

Place the pumpkin on a baking tray. Drizzle on the oil or fat and season with a little fish sauce or salt, then toss to coat evenly. Arrange the pumpkin in a single layer on the tray and roast for 50–55 minutes, or until tender.

Meanwhile, to make the satay sauce, combine the macadamias and almond butter in the bowl of a food processor and pulse until ground. Add the ginger and chilli and process to combine. Add the tamari or coconut aminos, sesame oil and maple syrup and whiz, then gradually pour in 100 ml of water and pulse until the sauce is smooth. If the sauce is a little too thick, simply add more water. Season with a little fish sauce or salt, if desired. Transfer the satay sauce to a saucepan over medium heat and stir constantly until heated through, adding a little more water if needed. Keep warm.

Arrange the pumpkin on a platter. Squeeze the lime juice over the top and season with more fish sauce or salt if needed. Scatter over the pumpkin seeds, chilli, green peppercorns (if using), coriander and Thai basil leaves. Drizzle over some of the satay sauce and serve the rest on the side.

Palakoora vepadu (fresh spinach sautéed with aromatics such as cumin seeds, fenugreek seeds, curry leaves and turmeric) is a staple in South Indian mess halls. Hopefully my version will become a new staple in your own kitchen as it is so yummy and so versatile, and can be served as a side dish or base for spiced prawns or fish or roasted or grilled meat.

PALAKOORA VEPADU

80 ml (⅓ cup) melted coconut oil
    or good-quality animal fat*
1½ onions, finely chopped
1 teaspoon cumin seeds
¼ teaspoon fenugreek seeds
15 curry leaves, roughly chopped
6 garlic cloves, finely chopped
2 teaspoons ground cumin
1½ teaspoons ground coriander
¼ teaspoon chilli powder,
    or to taste (optional)
1 teaspoon ground turmeric
2 teaspoons finely grated ginger
300 ml Chicken Bone Broth
    (page 312) or vegetable stock
4 large handfuls of baby spinach leaves
sea salt and freshly ground
    black pepper
lemon wedges, to serve

* See Glossary

Heat 3 tablespoons of oil or fat in a large frying pan over medium heat. Add the onion and cook for 6 minutes, or until softened and translucent. Stir in the cumin seeds and cook for 30 seconds, or until the seeds start to pop. Add the fenugreek seeds, curry leaves and garlic and cook for 2 minutes, stirring frequently, until the garlic is cooked through.

Next, add the ground spices and ginger to the pan and continue to cook for 30 seconds, or until fragrant. Stir in 100 ml of the broth or stock and bring to a simmer, then remove from the heat and keep warm.

Melt 2 teaspoons of the remaining oil or fat in a large saucepan over medium heat. Add half the spinach and half the remaining broth or stock and stir, then cover with a lid and cook for 2–3 minutes, or until the spinach is wilted. Season with salt and pepper. Repeat with the remaining oil or fat, spinach and broth or stock.

Gently fold the onion mixture through the spinach and squeeze over a little lemon juice to taste. Serve.

Serves 4 as a side

I have to say this is one of the most delicious dressings you'll ever make. It enhances the humblest of vegetables, making them the star on any table. You can pretty well serve this dressing with any vegetable you like: okra, broccoli, brussels sprouts, zucchini, mushrooms, pumpkin, eggplant ... the list goes on. I like to get a bit of colour on my vegetables and add a roasted flavour, as I feel that carries the dressing better. I love this dish alongside some steak or grilled fish.

ROASTED CAULIFLOWER WITH FISH SAUCE DRESSING

2 tablespoons coconut oil, melted
1 head of cauliflower (about 1 kg), cut into florets
sea salt and freshly ground black pepper
1 handful of coriander leaves, roughly chopped
1 handful of mint leaves

Fish sauce dressing
80 ml (⅓ cup) fish sauce
1 tablespoon finely chopped coriander roots and stalks
1 teaspoon finely grated ginger
2 tablespoons apple cider vinegar
2 garlic cloves, finely chopped
2 teaspoons coconut sugar
1–2 bird's eye chillies, thinly sliced (if you like it milder, use ½–1 long red chilli)
2 tablespoons lime juice, plus extra if needed

Preheat the oven to 200°C (180°C fan-forced). Line a baking tray with baking paper.

Drizzle the oil over the cauliflower and toss to coat. Scatter the cauliflower in a single layer over the prepared tray and season with salt and pepper. Roast for 15–20 minutes, or until the cauliflower is golden and tender.

Meanwhile, make the fish sauce dressing. In a bowl or large jar, combine all the ingredients with 3 tablespoons of water, then stir until the sugar dissolves. Taste and add a little more lime juice if necessary.

Combine the roasted cauliflower and dressing on a platter and toss well. Scatter over the herbs and serve.

Serves 4 as a side

I can't say enough about the health benefits of adding Asian greens to your diet. There is a mountain of information about these amazing veggies that will make you love them for more than just their delicious taste. For this dish, I have added a very moreish miso glaze to provide a depth of flavour that will have you dreaming about these greens long after you have devoured them. Serve this alongside some grilled fish or braised chicken legs and you have a wonderful meal.

MISO-GLAZED BOK CHOY

125 ml (½ cup) Dashi Broth (page 317)
   or Fish or Chicken Bone Broth
   (page 318 or 312)
2 tablespoons white (shiro) miso
   paste (see Note) or tahini
1 teaspoon fish sauce
4 bok choy, halved lengthways
2 tablespoons coconut oil or
   good-quality animal fat*
2.5 cm piece of ginger,
   cut into matchsticks
1 tablespoon sesame seeds
toasted sesame oil, to serve

* See Glossary

Heat the broth in a small saucepan over medium–low heat until just starting to simmer. Remove from the heat. Add the miso or tahini and whisk until smooth and creamy. Whisk in the fish sauce, then set aside until needed.

Next, blanch the bok choy in boiling water for 2 minutes, or until just tender. Drain well.

Melt the coconut oil or fat in a large frying pan over medium heat. Add the bok choy, cut-side down, and cook for 1 minute, or until golden, then flip over, scatter over the ginger and cook for another minute. Pour in the miso sauce, gently toss and cook for a further minute, or until the sauce is heated through.

Arrange the bok choy on plates or a platter and pour over the sauce remaining in the pan. Scatter over the sesame seeds and drizzle on a little sesame oil, then serve immediately.

Note
– I recommend using organic miso paste as most soy-based products are GMO. Use tahini instead if you're avoiding soy products.

Serves 4 as a side

This is a fun variation on the classic kung pao chicken that is loved the world over. The great news is that it is super easy to make at home. Serve this as a side dish or add some chicken, prawns or boiled eggs to create a more substantial meal. Whichever way you go, you will have a damned tasty vegetable dish to enjoy.

KUNG PAO CAULIFLOWER

80 ml (⅓ cup) melted coconut oil
    or good-quality animal fat*
1 head of cauliflower (about 1 kg),
    cut into florets
sea salt and freshly ground
    black pepper
3 red Asian shallots, thinly sliced
2–3 long red chillies, halved and
    deseeded (leave the seeds in
    if you like it extra spicy)
4 garlic cloves, thinly sliced
2 teaspoons finely grated ginger
2 spring onions, white and green
    parts separated, finely chopped
80 ml (⅓ cup) tamari or
    coconut aminos*
400 ml Chicken Bone Broth
    page 312), vegetable stock
    or water
1½ tablespoons chilli oil
1½ teaspoons toasted sesame oil
1 tablespoon coconut sugar
1 tablespoon apple cider vinegar
¾ teaspoon Sichuan peppercorns,
    toasted and finely ground
1 tablespoon tapioca flour,*
    mixed to a paste with
    3 tablespoons cold water
60 g pine nuts (activated if possible*),
    toasted

* See Glossary

Preheat the oven to 200°C (180°C fan-forced). Line a baking tray with baking paper.

Drizzle 2 tablespoons of coconut oil or fat over the cauliflower and toss to coat. Scatter the cauliflower in a single layer over the prepared tray and season with salt and pepper. Roast for 15–20 minutes, or until golden and tender.

Heat the remaining coconut oil or fat in a large frying pan over medium–high heat, add the shallot, chilli, garlic, ginger and the white part of the spring onion and stir-fry for about 2 minutes, or until fragrant. Stir in the tamari or coconut aminos, the broth, stock or water, the chilli oil, sesame oil, sugar, vinegar and Sichuan pepper and cook for 2 minutes. Stir in the tapioca paste and bring to the boil, then add the green part of the spring onion, the pine nuts and roasted cauliflower and stir-fry for 1 minute until the cauliflower is coated with the sauce. Season with salt and pepper if needed and serve.

Tip
– You can use chopped activated cashew nuts instead of the pine nuts if you like.

Serves 4 as a side

This dish, originating in Hong Kong, is usually a whole lot of fried crispy garlic served with seafood like prawns, bugs, lobster or pipis. I have found replacing the seafood with Asian veggies works extremely well. The crunchy garlic sure packs a punch and leaves a lingering taste on the palate. These greens are perfect teamed with roast pork or duck.

ASIAN GREENS WITH TYPHOON GARLIC

1 bunch of Chinese broccoli (gai lan), trimmed and halved
3 baby bok choy, halved lengthways
2 tablespoons tamari or coconut aminos*
1 teaspoon finely grated ginger
80 ml (⅓ cup) Chicken Bone Broth (page 312) or vegetable stock
1 teaspoon honey

Typhoon garlic
150 g garlic cloves (about 50), peeled
400 ml melted coconut oil
sea salt

* See Glossary

To make the typhoon garlic, place the garlic in the bowl of a food processor and process until finely chopped. Don't over-process as it will turn to mush. Combine the garlic and coconut oil in a saucepan over medium heat and cook, stirring constantly, for 5–10 minutes, or until the garlic is lightly golden and crispy. (The garlic can burn very quickly so remove the pan from the heat as soon as it turns pale golden.) Strain the garlic (reserve the oil), shaking off any excess oil. Drain on paper towel and season with salt.

Cook the Chinese broccoli and bok choy in boiling salted water for 3 minutes, or until tender. Drain well.

Meanwhile, combine the tamari or coconut aminos, ginger, broth or stock and honey in a small saucepan and bring to a simmer. Remove from the heat.

Arrange the greens in a serving dish, pour over the hot tamari broth and scatter over half of the typhoon garlic, or to taste. Leftover garlic and oil can be kept in a sterilised glass jar in the fridge for up to 1 month.

Tip
– Use the leftover garlic oil as a cooking oil for other recipes.

Serves 4 as a side

If there is a way to turn brussels sprouts into a smash hit for the whole family, it has to be this recipe. Caramelising the sprouts makes them super tasty, and teaming them with a delicious creamy miso sauce creates an element of umami. Start cooking them like this and you will realise why they are one of the yummiest veggies on the planet. You might like to serve the chilli flakes on the side so the family can add as much or as little as they like. Try these roasted brussels sprouts alongside some grilled salmon or steak.

ROASTED BRUSSELS SPROUTS WITH MISO

600 g brussels sprouts,
    trimmed and halved
2 tablespoons coconut oil or
    good-quality animal fat,* melted
sea salt and freshly ground
    black pepper
250 ml (1 cup) Chicken Bone Broth
    (page 312) or vegetable stock
chilli flakes, to serve

Miso sauce
3 tablespoons white (shiro) miso
    paste (see Note page 148) or tahini
2 teaspoons apple cider vinegar
1 garlic clove, finely chopped
1 teaspoon honey
100 ml Chicken Bone Broth (page 312)

* See Glossary

Preheat the oven to 200°C (180°C fan-forced).

Place the brussels sprouts in a bowl and add the oil or fat. Season with salt and pepper and mix to coat the sprouts with the oil or fat. Transfer the sprouts to a roasting tin and spread out to form a single layer. Roast, tossing the sprouts from time to time, for 20 minutes, or until lightly golden and charred around the edges. Pour in the broth or stock, stir and roast for a further 15–20 minutes, or until the sprouts are caramelised and tender.

Meanwhile, combine the miso sauce ingredients in a small saucepan. Bring to a gentle simmer over medium–low heat and cook, stirring, for 5 minutes, or until heated through.

To serve, drizzle the miso sauce over the brussels sprouts and sprinkle on the chilli flakes.

Serves 4

On my first trip to Thailand I had the pleasurable experience of eating a traditional larb gai. Since then I have recreated the dish many times using the same method, but always experimenting with different ingredients, such as pork, mushrooms, seafood, duck, lamb and beef. This cauliflower larb is great to serve if you have vegetarians over. You could add a fried egg on top to make this more substantial.

ROASTED CAULIFLOWER LARB

½ head of cauliflower (about 500 g), florets and stalks roughly chopped
2 tablespoons coconut oil or good-quality animal fat,* melted
1–2 long red chillies, deseeded and sliced (leave the seeds in if you like it spicy)
150 g green beans, trimmed and roughly chopped
4 red Asian shallots, finely chopped
3 tablespoons lime juice
1½ tablespoons fish sauce or coconut aminos,* plus extra if needed
4 spring onions, green part only, thinly sliced
1 handful of mint leaves, torn
1 handful of Vietnamese mint leaves, torn
1 large handful of coriander leaves, torn
1 small handful of Thai basil leaves, torn
1 handful of bean sprouts, trimmed
sea salt (optional)
3 tablespoons sesame seeds, toasted

To serve
cabbage leaves, trimmed
2 Lebanese cucumbers, cut lengthways into wedges

* See Glossary

Preheat the oven to 240°C (220°C fan-forced). Line a baking tray with baking paper.

Place the cauliflower in the bowl of a food processor and pulse into small pieces.

Tip the cauliflower onto the prepared tray. Drizzle on 1 tablespoon of oil or fat, mix well and spread out to form a single layer. Roast, stirring with a spatula once or twice, for 10 minutes, or until golden.

Heat the remaining oil or fat in a wok or large saucepan over medium heat, add the chilli, beans and shallot and stir-fry for 2 minutes, or until fragrant. Next, add the roasted cauliflower rice, stir-fry for 2 minutes, then stir in the lime juice, fish sauce or coconut aminos, spring onion, mint, Vietnamese mint, coriander, Thai basil and bean sprouts. Taste and add some extra fish sauce, coconut aminos or salt if needed.

Sprinkle on the sesame seeds for a nice crunchy texture and serve in the cabbage leaves with the cucumber wedges on the side.

Serves 2–4 as side

We all know the story of having a whopping amount of celery on hand and not knowing what to do with it all. I wanted to share with you a wonderful recipe that will take care of any celery issues in your kitchen. This simple stir-fry is perfect with seared prawns or grilled or steamed fish, or, to turn it into a main meal, you might like to add some sliced pork or chicken when you are stir-frying.

CELERY STIR-FRY

2 tablespoons coconut oil or
   good-quality animal fat*
8 celery stalks, cut into
   10 cm × 1 cm batons
10 garlic cloves, thinly sliced
1–2 long red chillies, thinly sliced
200 g oyster mushrooms, torn
1 bunch of choy sum, trimmed
   and roughly chopped
sea salt and freshly ground
   black pepper (optional)
coriander sprigs, to serve

Ginger sauce
2 tablespoons tamari or
   coconut aminos*
80 ml (⅓ cup) Chicken Bone Broth
   (page 312), vegetable stock
   or water
½ teaspoon freshly ground
   black pepper
2.5 cm piece of ginger,
   cut into matchsticks
1 teaspoon toasted sesame oil

* See Glossary

Combine the ginger sauce ingredients in a small bowl and set aside.

Heat the oil or fat in a wok or large saucepan over medium–high heat until just starting to smoke. Add the celery, toss and stir-fry for 2 minutes, or until the celery is just starting to colour. Add the garlic and chilli and stir-fry for 30 seconds, or until fragrant. Add the oyster mushrooms and choy sum and continue to toss and stir-fry for 2 minutes, or until the garlic is starting to turn golden.

Push the veggies away from the centre of the pan and, working quickly, pour in the sauce. When the sauce starts to boil, combine with the veggies and cook, stirring, for 2–4 minutes, or until the veggies are just cooked through. Season with salt and pepper, if desired. Transfer the stir-fry to a serving platter, scatter over the coriander and serve.

Serves 2–4 as a side

The secret to making any vegetable shine comes down to the sauce, dressing or condiment you serve with it. A dressing like this ginger and miso number can be whipped up in no time to turn your humble vegetables into superheroes. Using greens like broccolini and spinach and adding the refreshing and slightly bitter crunch of radish make this a memorable dish for all the right reasons. This is perfect served alongside some grilled seafood or seared steak.

STEAMED BROCCOLINI AND SPINACH WITH GINGER–MISO DRESSING

2 bunches of broccolini, trimmed
2 teaspoons olive oil
sea salt and freshly ground
    black pepper
1 bunch of English spinach, trimmed
4 radishes, thinly sliced
1 spring onion, thinly sliced
2 toasted nori sheets,* chopped
2 big pinches of toasted
    sesame seeds

Ginger–miso dressing
1 tablespoon white (shiro) miso paste
    (see Note page 148) or tahini
1 teaspoon tamari or coconut aminos*
½ teaspoon coconut sugar
1 teaspoon apple cider vinegar
125 ml (½ cup) Chicken Bone
    Broth (page 312)
2 cm piece of ginger,
    cut into matchsticks
1 garlic clove, chopped
1 tablespoon olive oil

* See Glossary

Place the broccolini in a single layer in a steamer basket over a saucepan of boiling water. Cover and steam for about 5 minutes, or until the broccolini is tender. Transfer to a bowl, then add 1 teaspoon of olive oil, sprinkle on some salt and pepper and toss. Cover to keep warm and set aside.

Next, add the spinach to the steamer basket in a single layer and steam for about 1 minute, or until wilted. Place in another bowl, toss with the remaining olive oil and season with salt and pepper.

Meanwhile, to make the ginger–miso dressing, place the miso or tahini, tamari or coconut aminos, coconut sugar, vinegar, broth, ginger and garlic in a saucepan over medium heat. Bring to a simmer, then reduce the heat to low and cook, stirring occasionally, for 5 minutes, or until the ginger is tender and fragrant. Remove from the heat and whisk in the olive oil.

To serve, arrange the steamed spinach and broccolini on a serving platter. Scatter over the radish, then pour on the warm dressing. Serve with the spring onion, nori and sesame seeds sprinkled over the top.

Serves 4 as a side

Also known as white radish, daikon is a staple in Japanese cuisine. If you eat sashimi, often very thin strands of daikon are served underneath the sliced fish. Interestingly, the daikon helps to break down the protein when you eat the fish, making for a great pairing on a flavour and nutritional level. I have put my own spin on this by adding daikon to a stir-fry. Serve alongside any type of animal protein.

SAUTÉED DAIKON WITH GARLIC

2 tablespoons coconut oil
6 garlic cloves, finely chopped
2 tablespoons tamari or
    coconut aminos*
125 ml (½ cup) Chicken Bone
    Broth (page 312), vegetable
    stock or water
1 daikon (about 500 g), cut into
    finger-sized batons
2 tablespoons finely snipped garlic
    chives, tops reserved and snipped
    into 5 cm lengths to serve
½ teaspoon chilli flakes
    (add more if you like it spicy)
1 lemon wedge
2 teaspoons toasted sesame oil

* See Glossary

Melt the coconut oil in a large frying pan over medium heat. Add the garlic and cook, stirring occasionally, for 1–1 ½ minutes, or until just starting to colour. Increase the heat to medium–high, immediately add the tamari or coconut aminos and the broth, stock or water and stir to combine, then add the daikon and sauté for 3 minutes. Add the finely snipped garlic chives and the chilli flakes and continue to sauté for about 4 minutes, or until the daikon is just tender. Squeeze over a little lemon juice to taste.

To serve, arrange in a large bowl or on a platter, scatter over the garlic chive tops and finish with a drizzle of sesame oil.

Serves 4 as a side

Pkhali is a traditional Georgian dish of chopped and minced vegetables. In this case I have used just spinach and combined it with ground walnuts, vinegar, onion, garlic and herbs. Use as a dip for crackers and raw vegetables, spread onto toast or serve under a lovely piece of fish or meat. However you like to serve it, you will appreciate the complex flavours and textures this dish delivers.

SPINACH AND WALNUT PKHALI

400 g baby spinach leaves
1 handful of coriander leaves
1 handful of flat-leaf parsley leaves
80 g walnuts (activated if possible*), toasted
¼ teaspoon chilli powder
¼ teaspoon ground turmeric
1 teaspoon ground coriander
½ teaspoon ground fenugreek
3 tablespoons extra-virgin olive oil, plus extra to serve
2 tablespoons white wine vinegar or apple cider vinegar, or to taste
1 garlic clove, finely chopped
¼ onion, chopped
½ tablespoon lemon juice
sea salt and freshly ground black pepper
80 g pomegranate seeds

* See Glossary

Bring a large saucepan of salted water to the boil. Add the spinach, coriander leaves and parsley and cook for about 30 seconds, or until wilted. Drain, then immediately transfer the blanched greens to a bowl of iced water. When cold, drain again, then squeeze out as much water as possible.

Place the blanched greens in the bowl of a food processor and blend for about 1 minute, or until finely chopped. Transfer to a bowl and set aside.

Place the walnuts, chilli powder, turmeric, ground coriander, fenugreek, olive oil, vinegar, garlic, onion and lemon juice in the food processor and blend to a paste.

Add the spinach mixture to the food processor, season with salt and pepper and pulse a few times to combine with the paste. Transfer to a platter. Scatter the pomegranate seeds over the top, drizzle on a little more olive oil and serve.

Serves 4 as a side

Eggplant is a marvellous ingredient that lends itself to a multitude of cooking techniques, including roasting, deep-frying, sautéing, braising and steaming. Steaming eggplant is one of the easiest ways to prepare it and you can make a big batch with very little preparation. Here is a delicious recipe that combines soft eggplant flesh with nutty, creamy and earthy tahini. This makes a wonderful side dish to roasted pork belly, steamed fish or barbecued chicken skewers.

CHINESE-STYLE STEAMED EGGPLANT

5 Japanese eggplants (about 1 kg), stalks removed and halved lengthways
sea salt and freshly ground black pepper
½ bunch of Chinese broccoli (gai lan) or English spinach, trimmed
2 tablespoons olive oil
1 tablespoon sesame seeds, toasted
2 tablespoons garlic chives, finely snipped

Soy and sesame dressing
3 tablespoons tamari or coconut aminos*
3 tablespoons Chicken Bone Broth (page 312) or water
2 tablespoons apple cider vinegar
1 tablespoon unhulled tahini or Chinese sesame paste
1 teaspoon honey
1 teaspoon chilli oil, plus extra to serve (optional)
1 garlic clove, finely grated
1 teaspoon toasted sesame oil

* See Glossary

Place the eggplant in a single layer in a steamer basket over a saucepan of boiling water, then cover and steam for 15–20 minutes, or until the eggplant is tender. Remove from the steamer and sprinkle over a pinch of salt and pepper. Cover and set aside, keeping warm.

Next, add the Chinese broccoli or English spinach to the steamer basket in a single layer, sprinkle over a pinch of salt and pepper, then cover and steam for about 1–2 minutes, or until wilted.

Combine the soy and sesame dressing ingredients in bowl and whisk well.

When ready to serve, gently mix the eggplant and Chinese broccoli or English spinach with the olive oil to lightly coat. Drizzle over the dressing and scatter on the sesame seeds and garlic chives. Add more chilli oil, if desired, and serve.

Serves 4

Out of all the Indian street foods, you would be hard pressed to find anything as tantalising as the onion bhaji. Bhaji translated means 'fritter' and though onion might not be the first vegetable that jumps to mind when you think of fritters, these are so amazing they will become a firm family favourite. You can serve these on their own, with a little Indian pickle or chutney – like my piccalilli (page 275) or chow chow (page 271) – or with a simple minted mayo as I have done here.

ONION BHAJIS WITH MINTED MAYONNAISE

600 g red onions, thinly sliced
1½ teaspoons fine sea salt
1 long green chilli, halved,
    deseeded and chopped
1 tablespoon chopped coriander leaves
4 eggs
2 tablespoons tapioca flour*
2 tablespoons coconut flour
1 teaspoon baking powder
1 tablespoon curry powder
1½ teaspoons ground cumin
1½ teaspoons ground coriander
¼ teaspoon chilli powder or a pinch
    of cayenne pepper (optional)
sea salt and freshly ground
    black pepper
500 ml (2 cups) olive oil or
    melted coconut oil

Minted mayonnaise
200 g Mayonnaise (page 320)
1 tablespoon chopped mint

To serve
mint leaves
coriander leaves

* See Glossary

To make the minted mayonnaise, combine the mayo and mint in a bowl and mix well. Set aside until needed.

Place the onion in a colander, sprinkle with the salt and mix to combine. Leave the onion to sweat for 15 minutes, then squeeze all the moisture from the onion with your hands. (You can also wrap the onion in a clean tea towel or some cheesecloth and twist to squeeze out the liquid.)

Combine the onion, chilli, coriander leaves, eggs, tapioca and coconut flours, baking powder, curry powder, ground spices and chilli powder or cayenne pepper (if using) in a bowl and mix well to form a thick batter. Season with salt and pepper.

Heat the oil in a large, deep frying pan over medium heat. Test the heat of the oil by placing a small amount of batter in the pan. If the oil begins to sizzle around the batter, it has reached its ideal heat. Gently drop 1 tablespoon of batter per bhaji into the pan (don't cook more than four per batch) and cook for 1½–2 minutes on each side, or until golden brown and cooked through. You should get about 20 bhajis. Remove the bhajis from the pan using metal tongs or a slotted spoon and drain on paper towel. Sprinkle with salt and allow the bhajis to cool for 1 minute before serving with the minted mayonnaise and a few mint and coriander leaves.

Serves 4 as a side

If you have ever had the good fortune to grow your own spring onions, you will notice that they are one of the most generous plants – they just keep on giving. And that is why I love to prepare dishes like this, where one vegetable is celebrated in all its glory. Spring onions, like all onions, love to be kissed by flames or the heat of a grill; when lightly charred, they really come alive and bring so much to the palate. Here, I have teamed them with a simple Asian dressing that works a treat. Try serving alongside some grilled fish or steak.

CHARRED SPRING ONIONS WITH GINGER AND TAMARI

2 tablespoons coconut oil or
    good-quality animal fat*
2 bunches of spring onions
    (about 20), trimmed
toasted sesame seeds, to serve

Ginger and tamari dressing
2.5 cm piece of ginger,
    cut into matchsticks
1 garlic clove, finely chopped
3 tablespoons tamari or
    coconut aminos*
2 ½ tablespoons Chicken Bone
    Broth (page 312), vegetable
    stock or water
1 teaspoon honey
1 teaspoon toasted sesame oil

* See Glossary

Place all the ginger and soy dressing ingredients in a small saucepan and mix to combine. Bring to a simmer over medium heat, then reduce the heat to low and cook for 5 minutes, or until the ginger is softened. Remove from the heat and keep warm.

Meanwhile, heat a barbecue hotplate or chargrill pan to hot and brush with the oil or fat. Add the spring onions and cook for 30 seconds on all sides, or until soft and charred.

Place the spring onions on a serving platter. Pour over the ginger and soy dressing, sprinkle on the sesame seeds and serve immediately.

Serves 4

Miso-glazed eggplant is one of the most famous dishes in Japanese cuisine. The beauty of this dish is twofold: the umami flavour from the sweet miso entices you back for more and more and more; and the texture of the cooked eggplant is second to none. Remember when cooking eggplant that more is better (undercooked eggplant is not an enjoyable experience); always make sure it is cooked until tender and melting in the mouth. Having a slightly crispy skin also works wonders.

MISO-GLAZED ROASTED EGGPLANT WITH DASHI

300 ml Dashi Broth (page 317)
2 teaspoons tamari or coconut aminos*
2 eggplants, trimmed, halved
    lengthways and skin scored
    with a sharp knife in a crisscross
    pattern 2 cm apart
2 tablespoons coconut oil or
    good-quality animal fat,* melted

Miso glaze
1 tablespoon honey
1 tablespoon tamari or coconut aminos*
1 teaspoon apple cider vinegar
1 tablespoon olive oil
1 teaspoon sesame oil
2 tablespoons white (shiro) miso paste
    (see Note page 148) or tahini

To serve
1 quantity Crispy Garlic (page 315)
1 small handful of shiso leaves
1 small handful of bonito flakes*
2 pinches of black sesame seeds
a few drops of toasted sesame oil

* See Glossary

Preheat the oven to 220°C (200°C fan-forced).

Place the dashi broth and tamari or coconut aminos in a small saucepan and heat, stirring, until the broth is warm. Remove from the heat and set aside until needed.

To make the miso glaze, mix the honey, tamari or coconut aminos, vinegar, olive oil, sesame oil and miso or tahini in a bowl and set aside until needed.

Brush the cut sides of the eggplant with the oil or fat and place, cut-side down, on an oiled baking tray. Roast, flipping over halfway through, for 20 minutes, or until tender when tested with a fork or chopsticks.

Set the oven to grill.

Smear the cut sides of the eggplant with the miso glaze, then grill for 3–4 minutes, or until the eggplant is golden and charred.

Evenly ladle the broth into warm bowls, then add the eggplant, crispy garlic, shiso leaves, bonito flakes and sesame seeds. Drizzle over the sesame oil and serve.

Serves 4 as a side

This, hands down, would have to be my favourite recipe in this book. Anyone who knows me understands that I have a bit of a thing for okra. When it is in season and you can get your hands on some, buy a whole lot and use it in stir-fries, curries, soups, salads and braised dishes, like this, that just ooze flavour. If you can't find okra, zucchini or green beans would work well as a substitute. This side works well paired with grilled fish or your favourite roast meat.

TOMATO-BRAISED OKRA WITH ZA'ATAR

2 tablespoons coconut oil
   or good-quality animal fat*
1 large onion, chopped
4 garlic cloves, thinly sliced
1 long red chilli, halved, deseeded
   and finely chopped
1½ tablespoons za'atar,* plus extra
   to serve
2 tablespoons tomato paste
600 g fresh okra pods, trimmed
400 g tomatoes, diced
400 ml Chicken Bone Broth
   (page 312) or vegetable stock
finely grated zest and juice
   of ½ lemon
sea salt and freshly ground
   black pepper
extra-virgin olive oil, to serve

* See Glossary

Heat the oil or fat in a large saucepan over medium heat. Add the onion and sauté for 5 minutes, or until softened and translucent. Add the garlic, chilli, za'atar and tomato paste and cook for 1 minute, or until fragrant. Next, stir in the okra, tomatoes, broth or stock and lemon zest and bring to the boil. Reduce the heat to medium–low and simmer for 30 minutes, or until the sauce has thickened and the okra is cooked through. Mix in the lemon juice and season with salt and pepper. Sprinkle over some extra za'atar, drizzle with olive oil and serve.

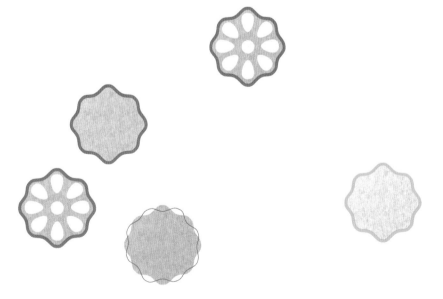

Serve 4–6

I bet everyone can remember the time they tried their first Thai green curry and what that amazing blend of spices and fat did to their tastebuds. I have made Thai green curry in many forms, from the classic chicken or prawn, to a veggie-filled version. When I feel like a fulfilling vegetable-based dish, this is the one for me. If you want an awesome meal, make some of the flatbreads on page 250 to serve with your curry and cauliflower rice. And of course you can add some prawns or chicken, if you like.

THAI GREEN CURRY

2 tablespoons coconut oil
1 onion, chopped
1 quantity Green Curry Paste
    (page 318)
200 ml coconut cream
300 g kent pumpkin, cut into
    2 cm chunks
200 g broccoli, cut into small florets
2 Japanese eggplants, halved
    lengthways and cut into
    2 cm pieces
2 kaffir lime leaves, torn
400 ml coconut milk
125 ml (½ cup) Chicken Bone Broth
    (page 312) or water
150 g button mushrooms, halved
100 g fresh okra pods, trimmed
7 asparagus spears, woody ends
    trimmed, cut into 4 cm pieces
100 g green beans, trimmed and halved
6–8 green peppercorn stalks in brine
    or 1½ tablespoons green
    peppercorns (optional)
1 tablespoon fish sauce,
    plus extra if needed
1 teaspoon coconut sugar,
    plus extra if needed
1 tablespoon lime juice,
    plus extra if needed
1 handful of Thai basil leaves
1 handful of coriander leaves
cooked Cauliflower Rice (page 312),
    to serve

Heat the coconut oil in a large saucepan or casserole dish over medium heat. Add the onion and sauté for 5 minutes, or until softened. Stir in the curry paste and cook for 4 minutes, or until fragrant and the spices and oil start to separate. Stir in the coconut cream and cook for a further 3 minutes, or until it separates.

Add the pumpkin, broccoli, eggplant and lime leaves to the pan, pour in the coconut milk and broth or stock and cover with a lid. Reduce the heat to medium–low and simmer, stirring occasionally, for 20 minutes to allow the curry sauce to develop in flavour.

Add the mushrooms, okra, asparagus, beans and green peppercorns (if using) to the pan and cook for a further 10–15 minutes, uncovered, until the vegetables are tender. Stir in the fish sauce, coconut sugar and lime juice. Taste and adjust the seasoning if needed with extra fish sauce, sugar and lime juice. Top the curry with the Thai basil and coriander leaves and serve with some cauliflower rice.

Serves 2–4 as a side

Mushrooms are once again being hailed as the ultimate superfood. I am not a huge fan of using the word superfood, as I believe all fruit, vegetables and animals are superfoods if they have been grown and raised or caught holistically and sustainably. That said, mushrooms are both nutritious and fascinating. Check out the book *Mycelium Running* by Paul Stamets to understand these amazing fungi more fully. Here, I have teamed some stir-fried mixed mushrooms with a green jalapeno dressing to add a little zing. This dressing is simply stunning with roasted cauliflower or with proteins like steak or grilled fish.

MUSHROOM STIR-FRY WITH JALAPENO DRESSING

2 tablespoons coconut oil or
　good-quality animal fat*
4 garlic cloves, finely chopped
2 spring onions, white and green
　parts separated, thinly sliced
sea salt and freshly ground
　black pepper
150 g shiitake mushrooms,
　whole if small, halved if large
150 g oyster mushrooms, torn
100 g shimeji mushrooms, trimmed
80 g wood ears, torn
70 g enoki mushrooms, trimmed

Jalapeno dressing
1 jalapeno chilli, half the seeds
　discarded, finely chopped
½ teaspoon grated garlic
80 ml (⅓ cup) apple cider vinegar
½ teaspoon fine sea salt
125 ml (½ cup) olive oil

* See Glossary

Place all the dressing ingredients in a blender and blend until smooth and emulsified. Set aside until needed.

Heat the oil or fat in a wok or large saucepan over medium–high heat until starting to sizzle. Add the garlic, white part of the spring onion and a pinch of salt and stir-fry for 15 seconds, or until fragrant. Add the shiitake and oyster mushrooms and stir-fry for 30 seconds. Next, add the shimeji mushrooms and wood ears and continue to stir-fry for 1 minute. Stir in the enoki mushrooms and cook for a further 10 seconds, or until the mushrooms are just tender. Season with salt and pepper.

Scoop the mushroom stir-fry onto a large platter, drizzle over the jalapeno dressing and sprinkle the green part of the spring onion over the top.

Tip
– You can use button mushrooms for this dish if that's all you have
　on hand.

Serves 4–6

I love a dish like this because you can pretty well throw in any vegetables you have in the fridge and, in no time at all, turn them into a scrumptious meal for the whole family. I advise doubling the recipe so you can eat some cold for breakfast or lunch or reheat for dinner the next day. If you wanted to add some animal protein, then prawns, fish, mussels, lamb or chicken would work a treat. Here, I serve it with cauliflower rice. Yum!

VEGETABLE MASALA

2 tablespoons coconut oil
1 onion, chopped
3 garlic cloves, finely chopped
8 curry leaves, chopped
1 long green chilli, halved,
    deseeded and thinly sliced
1 tablespoon finely grated ginger
1½ tablespoons finely chopped
    coriander leaves
500 ml (2 cups) coconut cream
1 tablespoon poppy seeds
50 g (⅓ cup) cashew nuts
    (activated if possible*), chopped
400 g diced tomatoes
    (see Note page 48)
125 ml (½ cup) Chicken Bone Broth
    (page 312) or water
1 carrot, diced
1 zucchini, diced
100 g green beans, cut into 4 cm batons
100 g broccoli florets
100 g eggplant, cut into 1.5 cm dice
100 g kent pumpkin, cut into 1.5 cm dice
sea salt and freshly ground
    black pepper

Spice mix
1 cinnamon stick
8 cloves
8 cardamom pods, crushed
1 teaspoon fennel seeds
2 teaspoons cumin seeds
2 teaspoons coriander seeds
1 teaspoon ground turmeric
½ teaspoon chilli powder

To serve
coriander leaves
cooked Cauliflower Rice (page 312)
lemon wedges

* See Glossary

To make the spice mix, toast the whole spices and seeds until fragrant, then grind in a spice grinder or with a mortar and pestle. Mix through the turmeric and chilli powder. Set aside until needed.

Melt the oil in a large saucepan over medium heat. Add the onion and cook for 5 minutes, or until softened. Stir in the garlic, spice mix and curry leaves and cook for about 30 seconds, or until fragrant. Add the chilli, ginger and chopped coriander and cook for 1 minute to soften, then stir in the coconut cream, poppy seeds, cashews, tomatoes and chicken broth or water. Mix well and bring to a simmer, then reduce the heat to low, cover with a lid and cook for 20 minutes to allow the flavours to develop. Add the carrot and cook for 10 minutes, then add the remaining vegetables, cover, and cook for a further 20 minutes, or until all the vegetables are tender. Season with salt and pepper.

Sprinkle the coriander leaves over the vegetable masala and serve with the cauliflower rice and a wedge or two of lemon to squeeze on top.

Comfort Food

Hasselback Sweet Potatoes with Salmoriglio/ Mixed Greens with Lemon Dressing/ Roasted Onions with Garlic and Thyme/ Artichokes à la Barigoule/ Roasted Pumpkin with Kimchi and Japanese Mayonnaise/ Braised Celery with Onion, Tomato and Pancetta/ Duck Fat–Roasted Jerusalem Artichokes with Watercress and Olives/ French Braised Peas with Cos Lettuce and Bacon/ Sautéed Asparagus with Garlic and Anchovy Dressing/ Blistered Green Beans with Tomato Pesto/ Braised French Onions/ Whole Roasted Broccoli with Tahini Dressing/ Kimchi-Loaded Sweet Potato Fries with Egg/ Roasted Brussels Sprouts with Dynamite Sauce/ Yellow Beans with Wilted Spinach and Radicchio/ Cabbage Roasted in Duck Fat/ Cumin-Roasted Dutch Carrots with Tahini Dressing/ Eggplant Parmigiana/ Grilled Zucchini and Broccolini with Caper Sauce/ Roasted Red Cabbage with Mustard Vinaigrette/ Curried Parsnip and Cauliflower Mash/ Grilled Cos with Anchovy and Garlic Dressing/ Roasted Red Onion Salad/ Roasted Pumpkin and Shallots with Sage/ Sweet and Sour Radicchio/ Roasted Zucchini with Spinach and Pesto/ Spiced Pumpkin and Cashew Soup/ Sweet Potato Wedges with Smoked Paprika Aioli/ Overcooked Veggies with Garlic and Chilli/ Roasted Butternut Pumpkin with Sumac Aioli

Serves 4 as a side

Hasselback sweet potatoes will become a firm favourite when you start serving these up for your family. The addition of a herbaceous sauce helps to lighten and lift the sweet potatoes, making them even more delectable. You can pack these in lunch boxes alongside some boiled eggs or cooked meat and a salad, or serve them with a roast dinner.

HASSELBACK SWEET POTATOES WITH SALMORIGLIO

4 sweet potatoes
2 tablespoons coconut oil or
    good-quality animal fat,* melted
2 tablespoons olive oil
2 teaspoons finely chopped
    thyme leaves
4 garlic cloves, finely grated
sea salt and freshly ground
    black pepper

Salmoriglio
3 garlic cloves, peeled
1 handful of oregano leaves
1 large handful of flat-leaf
    parsley leaves
100 ml extra-virgin olive oil
juice of 1 lemon

* See Glossary

Preheat the oven to 200°C (180°C fan-forced). Line a baking tray with baking paper.

Without cutting all the way through and stopping about 1 cm from the base, cut across each sweet potato at 5 mm intervals. (You can use two chopsticks to help here: place a chopstick along each long side of the sweet potato and then slice; the chopsticks stop you from cutting all the way through.) Carefully transfer the sliced sweet potatoes to the prepared tray.

Combine the coconut oil or fat, olive oil, thyme and garlic in a small bowl and season with salt and pepper.

Rub the garlic and thyme oil all over the sweet potatoes, getting it in between the slices, and bake for about 1 hour 20 minutes, or until the sweet potatoes are crispy on top and tender in the middle. (All sweet potatoes are different sizes so you may need a little longer.)

Meanwhile, to make the salmoriglio, pound the garlic and a pinch of salt to a paste using a mortar and pestle (or you can use a hand-held blender or food processor). Add the oregano and parsley, again pound to a paste, then stir in the olive oil and lemon juice. Season to taste with salt.

Sprinkle the hasselback sweet potatoes with extra salt, if desired, spoon over the salmoriglio and serve.

Serves 4 as a side

Truth be known, I don't always cook chef-inspired meals at home for the family. Sometimes I opt for the simplest of dishes to put on the table because I need to serve up quickly. At other times, I cook this way because it's what I feel like eating. Some good boiled veg with lemon and olive oil is simply exquisite. Serve with super fresh pan-fried fish and a side of kraut and you have a perfect family meal. Better still, it can be done in under 10 minutes!

MIXED GREENS WITH LEMON DRESSING

8 brussels sprouts, trimmed and halved
1 bunch of broccolini, trimmed
1 leek, pale part only, quartered
    lengthways, then cut into
    6 cm lengths
3 silverbeet leaves, leaves torn
    and stalks cut into 6 cm lengths
150 g sugar snap peas, stems
    and strings discarded
3 tablespoons extra-virgin olive oil
juice of 1 small lemon
sea salt and freshly ground
    black pepper
a couple of pinches of chilli
    flakes (optional)

Blanch each vegetable separately in boiling salted water until tender (about 5–6 minutes for the brussels sprouts and 2½–3½ minutes for the broccolini, leek, silverbeet and sugar snaps). Drain well and set aside, keeping warm. Alternatively, start with the veggies that take the longest and add the others as you go.

Meanwhile, place the olive oil and lemon juice in a small bowl and whisk to combine. Season with salt and pepper.

Arrange the boiled veggies in a serving bowl or on a platter, pour over enough lemon dressing to lightly coat and gently toss. Add the chilli flakes (if using) and more salt and pepper if needed and serve.

Serves 4–6 as a side

Once upon a time I saw onion only as a building block for flavour in sauces and braises. I would sweat down the onion with carrot and celery, then add some garlic and continue with the recipe. Lately, onion has become a favourite vegetable to serve as the star on the plate, alongside a good piece of grilled or roasted chicken, pork or fish. Just add some wilted spinach or kale and you have a meal fit for a queen or king.

ROASTED ONIONS WITH GARLIC AND THYME

80 ml (⅓ cup) melted duck fat or good-quality animal fat,* plus extra for greasing
6 onions, cut into 1 cm thick slices (use red, brown or sweet white onions)
sea salt and freshly ground black pepper
250 ml (1 cup) Chicken or Beef Bone Broth (page 312 or 310) or stock, plus extra if needed
3 rosemary sprigs
6 garlic cloves, thinly sliced
1 handful of thyme

* See Glossary

Preheat the oven to 190°C (170°C fan-forced). Lightly grease a roasting tin.

Arrange the onion slices in the prepared tin in a single layer. Brush the tops of the onion with half the fat and season with salt and pepper. Roast for 25 minutes, or until the onion starts to caramelise. Pour in the broth or stock, scatter on the rosemary and roast for a further 20 minutes, or until the onion is tender, adding more broth or stock if it dries out too quickly.

When the onion is ready, heat the remaining fat in a frying pan over medium heat. Add the garlic and fry for 1 minute, or until lightly golden. Add the thyme (taking care as the fat may spit) and fry for 30 seconds, or until the stalks look lightly golden. Remove from the heat and pour the garlic, thyme and fat from the pan over the onion. Serve.

Serves 4 as a side

When travelling in the south of France, you notice that the cuisine shows a great respect for and celebrates vegetables that are in season. One of my favourite dishes from this part of the world is the timeless classic, *artichokes à la barigoule* (braised globe artichokes). I love the way the aromatics and smoky bacon highlight the artichokes. Serve on the table alongside some grilled or roasted meat or fish.

ARTICHOKES À LA BARIGOULE

juice of 1 lemon
10 globe artichokes
2 lemons, quartered
2 tablespoons coconut oil or
    good-quality animal fat*
200 g speck or rindless bacon,
    finely diced
1 onion, finely chopped
2 carrots, finely diced
2 celery stalks, finely diced
3 garlic cloves, finely chopped
3 thyme sprigs
sea salt and freshly ground
    black pepper
250 ml (1 cup) dry white wine
    (such as chardonnay)
750 ml (3 cups) Chicken Bone Broth
    (page 312)
2 tablespoons extra-virgin olive oil
2 tablespoons chopped flat-leaf
    parsley leaves
½ lemon, to serve

* See Glossary

Fill a large bowl with 750 ml (3 cups) of water and add the lemon juice.

Trim the artichoke stalks to 3 cm. Peel away the tough outer leaves until you reach the soft, pale yellow inner leaves. Using a small sharp knife, trim away the tough green skin from the stalks so you are left with the pale yellow edible core. Working quickly, trim 2 cm from the pointed top of each artichoke, then cut in half lengthways and rub the artichoke flesh with a lemon quarter to prevent it from oxidising. Using a teaspoon, scope out the fibrous 'choke' in the centre and discard, then immediately squeeze on some more lemon juice. Place all the prepped artichokes in the lemon water and set aside until needed. Drain when ready to cook.

Heat the oil or fat in a large, deep frying pan over medium–high heat. Add the speck or bacon and sauté for about 5 minutes, or until lightly golden. Stir in the onion, carrot, celery, garlic and thyme, season with salt and pepper and cook for about 5 minutes, or until softened.

Pour the white wine into the pan and simmer until reduced by half. Add the broth and drained artichokes, reduce the heat to medium, cover with a lid and cook for about 25 minutes, or until the artichokes are tender when pierced with the tip of a knife. Season with salt and pepper if needed. Serve immediately, with a drizzle of olive oil and the parsley scattered over the top. Add a squeeze of lemon, if you desire.

Note
– You can use cooked artichokes in brine if fresh artichokes are not available. If using pre-cooked artichokes, you will only need half the amount of chicken bone broth and the cooking time should be reduced from 25 to 2 minutes.

Serves 4

This to me is basically a meal on its own. It's as easy as taking some amazing roasted pumpkin and topping it with goodies like fatty homemade mayo, kimchi for good gut health, toasted nori, smoky bonito flakes and crunchy sesame seeds. You could also add a fried egg with a runny yolk to add to the richness, or roasted chicken or smoked fish.

ROASTED PUMPKIN WITH KIMCHI AND JAPANESE MAYONNAISE

½ butternut pumpkin (about 500 g), seedless top part only
1 tablespoon coconut oil or good-quality animal fat*
sea salt and freshly ground black pepper
160 g Japanese Mayonnaise (page 319)
300 g Quick Kimchi (page 296)
1 nori sheet,* cut into matchsticks
1 small handful of bonito flakes* (optional)
1 tablespoon mixed black and white sesame seeds, toasted
1 tablespoon finely snipped chives
toasted sesame oil, to serve

* See Glossary

Preheat the oven to 200°C (180°C fan-forced). Line a baking tray with baking paper.

Cut the pumpkin into four rounds about 2 cm thick, then rub the cut sides with the oil or fat and season with salt and pepper. Place on the prepared tray in a single layer and roast for 20 minutes, then flip over and roast for a further 20 minutes, or until the pumpkin rounds are cooked through and golden. Set aside to cool slightly.

Place the roasted pumpkin on serving plates, spoon the mayonnaise over each round, then top with the kimchi. Sprinkle on the nori, bonito flakes (if using), sesame seeds and chives. Finish with a drizzle of sesame oil and a pinch of salt.

Serves 4

This is my take on a traditional pasta dish with sauce. My version replaces the pasta with braised celery, which is infinitely tastier and more nutritious. I have used pancetta but you could also try bacon or, if you like, bone marrow, salami, blood sausage or any other sausage to add a little richness to the dish.

BRAISED CELERY WITH ONION, TOMATO AND PANCETTA

2 tablespoons coconut oil or
   good-quality animal fat*
2 large onions, chopped
200 g pancetta, chopped
4 garlic cloves, thinly sliced
2 tablespoons tomato paste
125 ml (½ cup) dry white wine
   (such as chardonnay)
700 g celery stalks (about ½ bunch),
   cut into 6 cm lengths on the diagonal
   (reserve the leafy tops and leaves
   for another use)
400 g whole peeled tomatoes, crushed
   (see Note page 48)
250 ml (1 cup) Chicken or Beef Bone
   Broth (page 312 or 310), vegetable
   stock or water
1 teaspoon dried oregano
sea salt and freshly ground
   black pepper
finely grated zest of 1 lemon
1 handful of basil leaves

* See Glossary

Heat the oil or fat in a large, heavy-based saucepan over medium heat. Add the onion and pancetta and sauté for 10 minutes, or until the onion is starting to caramelise.

Next, add the garlic and tomato paste to the pan, stir well and cook for 2 minutes, or until fragrant. Pour in the wine, then cook until the liquid has almost evaporated. Stir in the celery, crushed tomatoes, broth, stock or water and dried oregano and bring to the boil. Reduce the heat to medium–low, cover with a lid and cook for 40 minutes. Remove the lid and cook for a further 20 minutes, or until the celery is tender and the sauce is reduced by half. Season with salt and pepper.

To serve, sprinkle on the lemon zest and basil.

Serves 4–6

Roasting Jerusalem artichokes is, without doubt, the best way to serve these amazing vegetables. And I would go so far as to say that I don't think any other vegetable tops them when it comes to flavour and textural delight. I have kept this super simple and added some olives, shallots and watercress to create a pretty amazing salad that works as a stand-alone dish with some soft-boiled eggs or as a side served with roasted pork or chicken or grilled fish.

DUCK FAT–ROASTED JERUSALEM ARTICHOKES WITH WATERCRESS AND OLIVES

sea salt and freshly ground
    black pepper
1 kg Jerusalem artichokes, skin on,
    cut into 2.5 cm pieces
6 French shallots, quartered
1 garlic bulb, kept whole
80 ml (⅓ cup) melted coconut oil
    or good-quality animal fat*
1 large handful of watercress
    sprigs, trimmed
200 g kalamata olives, pitted

Balsamic dressing
1½ tablespoons balsamic vinegar
    or coconut aminos*
3 tablespoons extra-virgin olive oil

* See Glossary

Preheat the oven to 180°C (160°C fan-forced). Line a large roasting tin with baking paper.

To make the dressing, place the vinegar or coconut aminos and the olive oil in a bowl and whisk to combine. Season with a pinch of salt and pepper. Set aside until needed.

Place the artichoke, shallot and garlic bulb in the prepared tin, add the oil or fat and toss to coat. Season with salt and pepper and roast for 55–65 minutes, or until the artichoke is tender inside and crispy on the outside and the garlic is softened and golden. Remove the garlic and set aside to cool a little.

Transfer the roasted artichoke and shallot to a bowl.

When cool enough to handle, cut the garlic cloves in half, squeeze the soft flesh from the skins over the artichoke and shallot and gently toss through. Season with salt and pepper if needed. Toss through the watercress and olives, then arrange in a serving dish and drizzle over the dressing.

Serves 4–6 as a side

One of the best ways to make peas shine is to prepare them French-style (*petits pois à la Française*). Served in this fashion, the peas make for a substantial meal. This dish is also a sensational accompaniment to poached, fried or soft-boiled eggs, braised or roasted lamb, or steamed or grilled fish.

FRENCH BRAISED PEAS WITH COS LETTUCE AND BACON

3 tablespoons coconut oil or
    good-quality animal fat*
1 large onion, chopped
220 g rindless bacon rashers, chopped
4 garlic cloves, thinly sliced
1 bay leaf
4 thyme sprigs, leaves picked
    and chopped
150 ml dry white wine
    (such as chardonnay)
600 ml Chicken Bone Broth (page 312)
250 g fresh or frozen peas
2 baby cos lettuces, halved lengthways
sea salt or freshly ground black pepper
½ teaspoon lemon juice,
    or to taste (optional)

* See Glossary

Heat 2 tablespoons of oil or fat in a large saucepan over medium heat. Add the onion and sauté for 8 minutes, or until it is just starting to colour. Next, add the bacon and fry for about 5 minutes, or until golden. Stir in the garlic, bay leaf and thyme and cook for a further 1 minute, or until fragrant.

Pour the wine into the pan, stir well and simmer for 2½–3 minutes, or until reduced by half. Stir in the broth. Bring to a simmer, then reduce the heat to medium–low and cook for 15 minutes to allow the flavours to infuse.

Next, add the peas to the pan and gently simmer for 20 minutes, or until they are tender.

Meanwhile, heat the remaining oil or fat in a large frying pan over medium–high heat. Add the lettuce halves, cut-side down, and cook for 1–2 minutes until golden brown, then flip over and cook for a further 1–2 minutes. Take care as the oil may spit. Season with salt and pepper.

Add the lettuce to the pea-braising broth and season with salt and pepper if needed. Cover with a lid and cook for 3 minutes, or until the lettuce wilts. Squeeze over some lemon juice, if you like, and serve.

Serves 4 as a side

In spring, when asparagus comes into season, there is a bit of excitement in the restaurant world as it marks the end of the colder months and the start of being able to focus on lighter ingredients. Asparagus has long been considered the darling of the vegetable kingdom but it can be quite expensive. When it is abundant and the price drops, a celebratory dish like this is one to behold. This simple preparation works a treat alongside grilled or steamed fish, steak, roasted chicken or pork, or eggs any way you like.

SAUTÉED ASPARAGUS WITH GARLIC AND ANCHOVY DRESSING

1 lemon, halved
3 tablespoons coconut oil or
    good-quality animal fat*
3 bunches of asparagus,
    woody ends trimmed
sea salt and freshly ground
    black pepper
6 garlic cloves, chopped
4 salted anchovy fillets, rinsed,
    patted dry and finely chopped
1–2 long red chillies, halved,
    deseeded and finely chopped
2 tablespoons finely chopped
    flat-leaf parsley leaves
finely grated zest of ½ lemon
80 ml (⅓ cup) olive oil
1 handful of flaked almonds, toasted

* See Glossary

Heat a small frying pan over high heat. Dry-fry the lemon halves, cut-sides down, for 2–5 minutes, or until charred. Set aside.

Heat a large frying pan over medium–high heat, add 1 tablespoon of oil or fat, then add the asparagus and cook, tossing, for 3–3 ½ minutes, or until golden and lightly charred. Season with salt and pepper. Remove from the pan and set aside.

Wipe the pan clean and heat the remaining oil or fat over medium heat. Add the garlic and cook for 30–40 seconds, or until it just starts to colour. Next, add the anchovy and chilli and cook for 15 seconds, or until fragrant.

Return the asparagus to the pan, add the parsley and cook, tossing, for about 30 seconds, or until the asparagus is almost cooked through but still slightly crisp in the middle. Remove from the heat, add the lemon zest, squeeze over the lemon juice and add the olive oil, and give the pan another good toss. Season with salt and pepper if needed.

Arrange the asparagus in a serving dish and spoon over the garlic and anchovy dressing. Sprinkle over the toasted almonds and serve with the charred lemon halves for squeezing.

Serves 4 as a side

Green beans are a wonderful and very versatile vegetable, as they team well with all types of seafood and meat. When you want to make them the star of your plate, all you need to do is toss them with a delicious dressing or pesto, which gives them body and adds a lovely richness and depth of flavour. Marry these beans with grilled fish, roasted chicken legs or lamb cutlets.

BLISTERED GREEN BEANS WITH TOMATO PESTO

sea salt and freshly ground
    black pepper
2 tablespoons coconut oil or
    good-quality animal fat*
2 garlic cloves, finely chopped
600 g green beans, trimmed
200 g cherry tomatoes, halved
1 large handful of basil leaves, torn

Tomato pesto
300 g semi-dried tomatoes
    (store-bought or see page 322
    for a recipe)
½ tomato, chopped
80 g (½ cup) almonds (activated
    if possible*), chopped
1 garlic clove, chopped
2 tablespoons red wine vinegar
    or apple cider vinegar
½ teaspoon smoked paprika
70 ml extra-virgin olive oil

* See Glossary

To make the tomato pesto, place the semi-dried tomatoes in the bowl of a food processor and add the tomato, almonds, garlic, vinegar and paprika. Pulse until combined but still slightly chunky. Add 2 tablespoons of water and pulse to combine. Transfer to a bowl, mix in the olive oil and season with salt and pepper. Set aside.

Heat the oil or fat in a wok or large frying pan over medium–high heat. Add the garlic, swirl around in the pan and cook for 10 seconds, or until fragrant. Add the beans and sauté, tossing occasionally, for 4–5 minutes, or until just starting to colour and blister. Stir in the cherry tomatoes and basil and sauté for 1½ minutes, or until softened. Stir in half the tomato pesto, toss through the beans and cook for a further 1 minute, or until heated through. Season with salt and pepper. Spoon the remaining pesto into a small serving bowl and pass at the table with the beans.

Tip
– Any leftover pesto can be stored in an airtight container in the fridge for 2–3 days and used as a dip, in sandwiches or to dress zucchini noodles.

Serves 4–6 as a side

Braising onions in good-quality broth or stock really brings out the sweetness in these very versatile and quite delicious vegetables.
To turn this into a magnificent meal, simply add some chicken thighs to the braising broth for the last 20 minutes of cooking or serve some grilled sausages on the side.

BRAISED FRENCH ONIONS

3 tablespoons duck fat or other good-quality animal fat* or coconut oil
600 g French shallots, peeled
600 g pickling onions, peeled
4 garlic cloves, chopped
2 teaspoons finely chopped thyme leaves
1 litre Beef or Chicken Bone Broth (page 310 or 312) or vegetable stock
2 bay leaves
sea salt and freshly ground black pepper
1 bunch of English spinach, trimmed (optional)
2 tablespoons finely snipped garlic chives
paleo bread, to serve (optional)

* See Glossary

Preheat the oven to 180°C (160°C fan-forced).

Melt the fat or oil in a large ovenproof casserole dish over medium–high heat. Add the shallots and pickling onions and cook, stirring occasionally, for 12 minutes, or until the shallots and onions are brown.

Reduce the heat to medium, add the garlic and thyme to the dish and cook for 1 minute. While stirring constantly, gradually pour in the broth or stock, then add the bay leaves. Bring to the boil, skimming off any scum that rises to the surface. Transfer to the oven to braise for 1 hour, or until the shallots and onions are cooked through and the broth is full of flavour with a nicely balanced sweetness. Season with salt and pepper to taste.

If using spinach, stir it into the dish, cover and return to the oven for a further 5 minutes, or until the spinach has wilted. Sprinkle the garlic chives over the top and serve with some paleo bread on the side, if desired.

Serves 4 as a side

Middle Eastern cuisine just screams of flavour and colour, with its clever combination of spices that dance on the palate and the textural component that provides contrast. For this memorable dish, I have teamed the ever-versatile broccoli with creamy tahini dressing and a jewel-like scattering of pomegranate seeds, mint and almonds. Serve as a side with your favourite roast meat or some grilled fish.

WHOLE ROASTED BROCCOLI WITH TAHINI DRESSING

1 large or 2 small heads of broccoli (about 500 g)
1 tablespoon coconut oil or good-quality animal fat,* melted
sea salt and freshly ground black pepper
375 ml (1½ cups) Chicken Bone Broth (page 312), vegetable stock or water
80 g pomegranate seeds
1 tablespoon toasted and roughly chopped almonds (activated if possible*)
1 handful of roughly chopped mint leaves
½ teaspoon sumac*

Tahini dressing
1 tablespoon hulled tahini
200 g Coconut Yoghurt (page 314)
½ teaspoon finely chopped garlic
1 tablespoon lemon juice, or to taste
pinch of baharat* or ground cumin
1½ tablespoons warm water, plus extra if needed

* See Glossary

Preheat the oven to 160°C (140°C fan-forced).

Remove any leaves and cut away the stalk from the base of the broccoli. Rub the broccoli with the oil or fat and season with salt and pepper.

Place the broccoli in a casserole dish, then pour in the broth, stock or water and cover with a lid. Roast, adding a little more liquid if it starts to look dry, for 40–45 minutes, or until the broccoli is tender.

Increase the oven temperature to 220°C (200°C fan-forced). Remove the lid and roast the broccoli for a further 5 minutes, or until slightly golden.

Meanwhile, to make the tahini dressing, combine the tahini, coconut yoghurt, garlic, lemon juice and baharat or cumin in a bowl, add the warm water and mix well, adding more water if needed. Season with salt to taste.

To serve, place the roasted broccoli on a serving dish, spoon on the tahini dressing, then scatter over the pomegranate seeds, almonds, mint and sumac.

Serves 2

Loaded fries have become super popular, and if you are wondering what they are, let me explain. The simple definition is they are fries that are loaded with extra goodness. Here, I have added kick-ass dynamite sauce (I find the mayo and chilli combination is perfect for sweet potato fries) topped with spicy kimchi and fried eggs. These last two ingredients elevate any meal, and the runny egg yolk helps turn this into a gooey but delicious mess of unbeatable flavour.

KIMCHI-LOADED SWEET POTATO FRIES WITH EGG

1 tablespoon coconut oil or
   good-quality animal fat,*
   plus extra for greasing
4 eggs
sea salt and freshly ground
   black pepper
100 g Quick Kimchi (page 296)
   or enough to your liking
100 g Dynamite Sauce (page 317)
1 spring onion, thinly sliced

Sweet potato fries

700 g sweet potatoes, cut into
   1 cm thick batons
50 g tapioca flour*
600 ml melted coconut oil or
   good-quality animal fat*

* See Glossary

To make the fries, dust the sweet potato with the tapioca. Heat the oil or fat in a large saucepan to 160°C. (To test the temperature, add a small piece of sweet potato. If small bubbles of oil appear at the edges, it's ready.) Add the sweet potato fries in three batches and cook for 3 minutes. Drain in a single layer on paper towel, then transfer to the fridge to chill for 1 hour, or the freezer for 15 minutes. Separate the fries after chilling and before deep-frying for the second time. Reheat the oil in the pan to 180°C. To check, place a piece of sweet potato in the oil and if it immediately bubbles quite vigorously, it's ready. Deep-fry the sweet potato fries in three batches for around 2–2½ minutes, or until golden and crisp. Remove with a slotted spoon, drain on paper towel and season with salt.

Melt the 1 tablespoon of oil or fat in a large frying pan over medium heat. Crack in the eggs and cook for 2–3 minutes, or until cooked to your liking. Season with salt and pepper. Keep warm.

To serve, divide the fries between two serving bowls. Top with the kimchi and fried eggs and drizzle on the dynamite sauce. Sprinkle on some spring onion and pepper and serve right away.

Tips

– The leftover deep-frying oil or fat can be strained and stored in an airtight container in the fridge to be reused.
– You could also simply roast sweet potatoes in the oven until tender and top accordingly.

Serves 4 as a side

A big bowl or platter of brussels sprouts served like this is appealing and satisfying on so many levels. The dynamite sauce (what you usually find in spicy tuna hand-rolls) is just a simple hot mayonnaise that works well with many different vegetables and proteins. I have also incorporated some furikake seasoning and nori seaweed to add a bit of umami flavour. These go perfectly with steak or grilled fish.

ROASTED BRUSSELS SPROUTS WITH DYNAMITE SAUCE

600 g brussels sprouts, trimmed
    and halved
3 tablespoons coconut oil or
    good-quality animal fat,* melted
sea salt and freshly ground
    black pepper
350 ml Chicken Bone Broth
    (page 312) or vegetable stock,
    plus extra if needed
½ spring onion, thinly sliced
170 g Dynamite Sauce (page 317)
1–2 tablespoons Furikake
    Seasoning (page 318)

* See Glossary

Preheat the oven to 200°C (180°C fan-forced).

Place the brussels sprouts in a bowl, add the oil or fat, season with salt and pepper and mix well. Transfer the brussels sprouts to a roasting tin, spread out to form a single layer and roast, tossing from time to time so they colour evenly, for 20 minutes, or until golden and charred. Pour in the broth or stock, stir with a spatula and cook for a further 10 minutes, or until the sprouts are tender. Add more broth or stock if it starts to dry out too quickly.

Meanwhile, stir the spring onion into the dynamite sauce, then pour into a small bowl and set aside until ready to use.

To serve, place the roasted brussels sprouts on a serving platter, spoon over some dynamite sauce and sprinkle on the furikake seasoning. Serve the remaining dynamite sauce on the side.

Serves 4

The motto of my home cooking is to include an array of vegetables that complement each other in a dish and then add a healthy piece of protein either to the dish or on the side. And that is why I love a recipe like this with its many different colour and flavour profiles, from bitter to peppery to sweet. Flake in some smoked trout or add some soft-boiled eggs to make this a substantial family meal.

YELLOW BEANS WITH WILTED SPINACH AND RADICCHIO

2 tablespoons duck fat or other good-quality animal fat* or coconut oil
1 onion, thinly sliced
4 garlic cloves, chopped
1 teaspoon finely chopped thyme leaves
300 g yellow beans, trimmed and halved
150 ml Chicken Bone Broth (page 312) or vegetable stock
50 g bone marrow flesh, chopped
½ bunch of English spinach, trimmed
1 head of radicchio, trimmed and leaves separated
1 teaspoon lemon juice, or to taste
sea salt and freshly ground black pepper
chilli flakes, to serve (optional)
extra-virgin olive oil, to serve (optional)

* See Glossary

Heat the fat or coconut oil in a large frying pan over medium heat. Add the onion and sauté for 5 minutes, or until just tender. Add the garlic and thyme and cook for 30 seconds, or until the garlic is fragrant. Add the beans and sauté for 2 minutes, then pour in the broth or stock and cook for a further 3 minutes, or until the beans are just tender. Remove from the pan and set aside, keeping warm.

Wipe the pan clean, add the bone marrow and cook for 1½ minutes, then stir in the spinach and sauté for 2 minutes, or until the spinach is wilted. Add the radicchio and return the beans and garlic to the pan, then drizzle over the lemon juice and toss for about 1 minute, or until the radicchio is just wilted. Season with salt and pepper, sprinkle on the chilli flakes and drizzle with olive oil, if desired, and serve.

Serves 4 as a side

This might look like the plainest dish in the whole book but I can honestly say that it is one of the most delicious. It is also the easiest, so I implore you to give it a go. I generally do this in the same tin that I am using to roast a chicken or some pork to capture all the delicious juices from the meat. Here, I have roasted the cabbage with duck fat, as I really don't think there is a better fat to cook with in terms of flavour. Serve this with any roasted meat or grilled seafood or top each cabbage slice with a fried egg.

CABBAGE ROASTED IN DUCK FAT

80 ml (⅓ cup) melted duck fat or
  coconut oil
1 small green or savoy cabbage,
  cut into 2 cm thick slices
250 ml (1 cup) Chicken Bone Broth
  (page 312)

Garlic salt
1 teaspoon garlic powder
1½ teaspoons fennel seeds, crushed
  using a mortar and pestle
½ teaspoon freshly ground
  black pepper
3 teaspoons sea salt

Place all the garlic salt ingredients in a small bowl and mix to combine.

Preheat the oven to 220°C (200°C fan-forced).

Heat a chargrill pan over medium–high heat. Brush the grill with some of the duck fat or coconut oil and grill the cabbage on both sides for 2–2½ minutes, or until charred.

Transfer the cabbage to a roasting tin and spread out to form a single layer. Drizzle over the remaining duck fat or coconut oil and season with a big pinch of garlic salt. Pour in the broth and roast for 17–20 minutes, or until the cabbage is cooked through.

To serve, place the roasted cabbage slices on a large platter, pour over the juices from the roasting tin and season with more garlic salt if needed.

Tip
– Store the leftover garlic salt in an airtight container in the pantry for up to 3 months.

Serves 4–6 as a side

I don't know about you, but whenever I see beautiful baby carrots at the market I just need to buy them and, usually, eat a couple right then and there. The ones that do make it home get split between the kids' lunch boxes or are used in a simple salad like this, which is the perfect accompaniment to roasted fish, pork or lamb.

CUMIN-ROASTED DUTCH CARROTS WITH TAHINI DRESSING

sea salt and freshly ground
    black pepper
30–35 heritage Dutch carrots, trimmed
2 tablespoons coconut oil or
    good-quality animal fat,* melted
1 teaspoon ground cumin
2 pinches of sumac*
1 handful of chopped mint leaves
1 handful of chopped flat-leaf
    parsley leaves

Tahini dressing
3 tablespoons hulled tahini
2 tablespoons lemon juice
1 garlic clove, finely grated (optional)

* See Glossary

To make the tahini dressing, place the tahini, lemon juice and garlic (if using) in a small bowl, add 3 tablespoons of water and mix to combine. Add a little salt to taste. Set aside.

Preheat the oven to 180°C (160°C fan-forced). Line a baking tray with baking paper.

Toss the carrots in the oil or fat and cumin, then season with salt and pepper. Scatter over the prepared tray in a single layer and roast, flipping the carrots halfway through, for 30 minutes, or until tender.

Drizzle the tahini dressing over the carrots, sprinkle on the sumac, mint and parsley and serve.

Serves 6

When you want a hearty vegetable dish to serve at a large family gathering, look no further than the delicious eggplant parmigiana. This makes for a lovely lunch or is a perfect addition to a roast dinner of any type.

EGGPLANT PARMIGIANA

4 large eggplants, cut lengthways
    into 1 cm thick slices
sea salt and freshly ground
    black pepper
100 ml melted coconut oil or
    good-quality animal fat*
1 quantity Italian Tomato Sauce
    (page 319)
2 handfuls of basil leaves, plus extra
    to serve
4 hard-boiled eggs, peeled and sliced
170 g Cashew or Macadamia
    'Cheese' (page 311 or 320)

* See Glossary

Preheat the oven to 200°C (180°C fan-forced). Line two large baking trays with baking paper.

Place the eggplant slices in a colander and mix through 1 tablespoon of salt. Allow to stand for 15 minutes for the bitter juices to drain. Rinse well and pat dry with paper towel.

Place the eggplant on the prepared trays in a single layer, brush with 90 ml of oil or fat and sprinkle on a little salt. Bake for 25 minutes, or until lightly golden.

Brush a 2 litre casserole dish with the remaining oil or fat and cover the base with a layer of eggplant, followed by a layer of tomato sauce and a scattering of basil leaves. Repeat this process until you have four layers, using the eggs in the centre layer. Scatter the nut 'cheese' over the top.

Reduce the oven temperature to 180°C (160°C fan-forced) and bake for 30 minutes, or until golden. Sprinkle over the extra basil leaves, finish with a grinding of black pepper and serve.

Serves 4 as a side

The flavoursome combination of grilled vegetables and a herbaceous sauce can never be underestimated. The sauce featured in this recipe is a bit of a go-to for me at home, as it works with pretty much everything that comes off the grill, whether it be seafood or pork, lamb or chicken, or vegetables of any sort. Always make sure when grilling leek that you give it long enough to cook through so it becomes tender and sweet.

GRILLED ZUCCHINI AND BROCCOLINI WITH CAPER SAUCE

2 leeks, white part only,
    halved lengthways
1 bunch of broccolini, trimmed
2 tablespoons coconut oil or
    good-quality animal fat,* melted
2 zucchini, quartered lengthways
sea salt and freshly ground
    black pepper
1 teaspoon chilli flakes (optional)

Caper sauce
finely grated zest and juice of 1 lemon
1 teaspoon Dijon mustard
100 ml extra-virgin olive oil
2 tablespoons finely chopped
    basil leaves
3 tablespoons finely chopped
    flat-leaf parsley leaves
1 teaspoon finely chopped
    oregano leaves
3 tablespoons salted baby capers,
    rinsed well, patted dry and chopped
3 anchovy fillets, finely chopped

* See Glossary

Preheat the oven to 200°C (180°C fan-forced).

Place the leek and broccolini in a steamer basket over a saucepan of simmering water, cover and steam for 3–4 minutes, or until tender. The broccolini should be just cooked through but still a little crunchy in the centre.

Heat a chargrill pan over medium–high heat. Brush the grill and the vegetables with the oil or fat and cook the vegetables, in batches, for 2–3 minutes on each side. Set the leek and broccolini aside and keep warm until needed.

Transfer the grilled zucchini to a baking tray in a single layer and season with salt and pepper. Cover with baking paper and cook for 8 minutes, or until tender.

Meanwhile, place all the caper sauce ingredients in a bowl, season with salt and pepper and mix well to combine.

Arrange the grilled veggies on a platter, sprinkle over the chilli flakes (if using) and drizzle over a generous amount of caper sauce. Serve.

Serves 4–6 as a side

Roasting has become one of my all-time favourite ways to prepare cabbage, as it is so easy and the end result is nothing less than extraordinary. Feel free to team your roasted cabbage with any dressing you have in the fridge and serve alongside your favourite roasted or braised meats.

ROASTED RED CABBAGE WITH MUSTARD VINAIGRETTE

1 red cabbage, cut through the
   core into 8 wedges
2 tablespoons coconut oil, melted
sea salt and freshly ground
   black pepper

Mustard vinaigrette
80 ml (⅓ cup) extra-virgin olive oil
2 tablespoons seeded mustard
1 garlic clove, finely grated
2 tablespoons apple cider vinegar
1 tablespoon honey

Preheat the oven to 180°C (160°C fan-forced). Line a large baking tray with baking paper.

Place the cabbage wedges, cut-side down, on the prepared tray, drizzle on the oil and season with salt and pepper. Cover with baking paper and roast for 1 hour. Increase the temperature to 220°C (200°C fan-forced). Remove the paper and continue to roast for 15 minutes, then flip the cabbage wedges over and cook for a further 15 minutes, or until golden.

Meanwhile, whisk all the mustard vinaigrette ingredients in a bowl until combined. Season with salt and pepper. Set aside.

Drizzle the vinaigrette over the roasted cabbage and serve.

Serves 6 as a side

Everybody loves mash. It was one of our first solid foods as babies and has made a regular appearance on our dinner plates ever since. The fact that it goes well with basically everything, tastes amazing and has a wonderful texture is hard to beat. The addition of Indian spices here is a fun take on a basic mash, and makes it perfect to accompany curried grilled snags, fish or roasted chicken, or to use as a topping for a spicy mince pie.

CURRIED PARSNIP AND CAULIFLOWER MASH

1 teaspoon yellow mustard seeds
1 teaspoon cumin seeds
1 garlic bulb, kept whole
80 ml (⅓ cup) olive oil, plus extra
    for drizzling
5 large parsnips (about 1 kg),
    peeled and core removed
1 head of cauliflower (about 1 kg),
    florets cut into 5 cm pieces
2 teaspoons lemon juice
1 tablespoon curry powder
2 tablespoons coconut cream
sea salt and freshly ground
    black pepper
2 Crispy Curry Leaves sprigs
    (page 315)

Preheat the oven to 180°C (160°C fan-forced).

Place the mustard and cumin seeds in a frying pan over medium heat and cook, tossing frequently, until fragrant and toasted. Set aside.

Place the garlic bulb on a baking tray, drizzle over some oil and roast for 35–40 minutes, or until golden and tender.

Meanwhile, bring a large saucepan of salted water to the boil. Add the parsnip and cauliflower and cook for 15–20 minutes, or until tender. Drain and shake off any excess water. Place the cooked parsnip and cauliflower in the bowl of a food processor. Cut the roasted garlic in half crossways and squeeze the soft garlic flesh straight into the food processor bowl. Add the 80 ml (⅓ cup) of oil, the lemon juice, curry powder and coconut cream and process until smooth. Season with salt and pepper to taste. Place the mash back in the pan over medium heat and stir constantly until heated through.

To serve, sprinkle the toasted mustard and cumin seeds over the mash and finish with the crispy curry leaves.

Serves 4 as a side

Lately, you may have noticed that grilled lettuce has become a bit of a trend. Always looking for new and interesting ways to present the best-quality produce, and using Chinese cuisine's stir-fried lettuce as inspiration, adventurous cooks are grilling lettuce, as well as cucumber and avocado, to redefine salads. This dish takes its cue from the famous Caesar salad and teams grilled baby cos with a delicious anchovy dressing. Enjoy as a side with some grilled fish, steak or roast lamb.

GRILLED COS WITH ANCHOVY AND GARLIC DRESSING

2 tablespoons coconut oil or
    good-quality animal fat*
4 baby cos lettuces, halved lengthways
sea salt and freshly ground
    black pepper
4 radishes, finely sliced (optional)
chilli flakes (optional)

Anchovy and garlic dressing
2 teaspoons coconut oil or
    good-quality animal fat*
8 garlic cloves, finely chopped
2 teaspoons finely chopped
    rosemary leaves
8 salted anchovy fillets, rinsed well,
    patted dry and finely chopped
3 tablespoons finely chopped
    flat-leaf parsley leaves
2 teaspoons finely grated lemon zest
1 tablespoon lemon juice
150 ml olive oil

* See Glossary

Heat a chargrill pan over medium–high heat. Brush the grill with the oil or fat and cook the cos, cut-side down, for 2–3 minutes, or until charred and slightly wilted. Turn the cos over and char the other side for 30 seconds. Transfer to a large serving platter and keep warm. Season with a little salt and pepper.

To make the anchovy and garlic dressing, melt the oil or fat in a small frying pan over medium heat. Add the garlic, rosemary and anchovy and cook for 1 minute, or until fragrant. Add the parsley, lemon zest, lemon juice and olive oil and stir to combine. Bring to a simmer, then remove from the heat and season to taste.

Drizzle the dressing over the cos and serve scattered with sliced radish and chilli flakes, if desired.

Serves 6–8 as a side

The key to roasting whole onions is to make sure they are cooked all the way through so they lose that bitter aftertaste and instead become meltingly sweet. You can serve this salad with your eggs in the morning or alongside any roasted meat in the evening. Onions are a wonderful form of prebiotic, which our good gut bacteria thrive on.

ROASTED RED ONION SALAD

6 red onions
100 ml melted coconut oil
    or good-quality animal fat*
sea salt and freshly ground
    black pepper
1 handful of oregano leaves

Balsamic dressing
2 tablespoons balsamic vinegar or
    coconut aminos*
80 ml (⅓ cup) extra-virgin olive oil

* See Glossary

Preheat the oven to 160°C (140°C fan-forced). Line a large baking tray with baking paper.

Peel the onions, leaving the bases intact. Cut each onion into six wedges, stopping about 1 cm from the base (this helps to keep the wedges intact).

Place the onion wedges on the prepared tray a few centimetres apart, then slightly open up the wedges by pushing them away from the centre with your fingers. They should look like a slightly closed flower. Drizzle the oil or fat in between and around the wedges and season with salt and pepper. Roast, basting with the juices occasionally, for 45–50 minutes, or until the wedges open into a flower and the petals are golden around the edges.

Meanwhile, mix the balsamic dressing ingredients together and season with salt and pepper.

Arrange the onion flowers on a serving platter, drizzle over the dressing and scatter over the oregano.

Serves 4 as a side

Pumpkin and sage are a classic combination in Italian cooking, and this simple recipe, served alongside a piece of fish, will liven up any dinner table. It also makes for a delicious packed school or work lunch with a chicken drumstick or lamb cutlet on the side.

ROASTED PUMPKIN AND SHALLOTS WITH SAGE

coconut oil or good-quality
    animal fat,* for greasing
1 kg kent pumpkin, peeled
    and cut into 3 cm pieces
8 French shallots, halved
15 garlic cloves, peeled
80 ml (⅓ cup) Garlic Confit oil
    (page 318) or melted coconut oil
    or good-quality animal fat*
3 teaspoons ras el hanout*
    or ground cumin
sea salt and freshly ground
    black pepper
200 ml Chicken or Beef Bone
    Broth (page 312 or 310)
    or vegetable stock
1 handful of sage leaves (about 20), torn
2 large handfuls of baby spinach leaves
1 small handful of pumpkin seeds
    (activated if possible*)

* See Glossary

Preheat the oven to 200°C (180°C fan-forced). Grease a large roasting tin with oil or fat.

Place the pumpkin, shallot and garlic in a bowl. Add 3 tablespoons of garlic confit oil, coconut oil or fat, season with the ras el hanout or cumin and salt and pepper and toss to coat.

Arrange the pumpkin, shallot and garlic in a single layer in the prepared tin, pour in the broth or stock and roast for 40–45 minutes, tossing halfway through, until the veggies are golden and tender.

When the veggies are almost done, heat the remaining garlic confit oil, coconut oil or fat in a wok or large, deep frying pan over medium heat. Add the sage leaves and cook for 30 seconds, or until fragrant. Add the spinach and sauté for a further 30 seconds, or until just wilted.

Toss the spinach and sage with the roasted veggies. Arrange on a platter, then sprinkle on the pumpkin seeds and serve.

Serves 4–6 as a side

Radicchio may not be everyone's favourite leafy vegetable as it does have a distinctly bitter taste, but it is this natural bitterness that I am so drawn to. Research has shown that the more bitter a leaf is, the more nutritional benefit it has for us, and it also helps to expand the palate and reduce sugar cravings. I see this recipe as a sort of training-wheels approach to eating radicchio – some sweetness is added to make it more palatable for the fussier eaters out there. This recipe is inspired by chef Josh Niland of seafood restaurant Saint Peter, who serves something very similar with a lovely piece of fish.

SWEET AND SOUR RADICCHIO

3 tablespoons coconut oil or
    good-quality animal fat*
1½ onions, sliced
2 tablespoons honey
125 ml (½ cup) apple cider vinegar
    or red wine vinegar
80 g golden raisins
sea salt and freshly ground
    black pepper
2 heads of treviso radicchio,
    cut into 4 wedges or
    1 large head of radicchio,
    cut into 8 wedges
2 tablespoons pine nuts (activated
    if possible*), toasted
2 tablespoons finely chopped
    flat-leaf parsley leaves

* See Glossary

Melt 2 tablespoons of the oil or fat in a large frying pan over medium–high heat. Add the onion and sauté for 8 minutes, or until softened and starting to caramelise. Stir in the honey, vinegar, 125 ml (½ cup) of water and the raisins and cook for a further 1 minute. Season with salt and pepper.

In another frying pan, heat the remaining oil or fat over medium–high heat. Add the radicchio, gently toss and cook for 3–5 minutes, or until just wilted, then pour in the onion sauce. Transfer to a serving dish, sprinkle on the pine nuts and parsley and serve.

Tip
– I like to serve this dish with roasted pork, duck or chicken,
   or grilled fish.

Serves 4 as a side

If you want to add some colour and flavour to your zucchini, then look no further than this amazing pesto that will make pretty much any vegetable come to life. I like to mix it through some simple greens, like spinach, as well as any pickled veg I have in the kitchen. This salad makes the perfect accompaniment to roasted chicken or lamb or any type of seafood dish.

ROASTED ZUCCHINI WITH SPINACH AND PESTO

4 zucchini, cut into 2 cm thick rounds
2 tablespoons coconut oil or
  good-quality animal fat,* melted
sea salt and freshly ground
  black pepper
2 large handfuls of baby spinach leaves
1 quantity Pickled Red Onion (page 85)

Pesto
2 large handfuls of basil leaves
2 large handfuls of flat-leaf
  parsley leaves
2 garlic cloves, roughly chopped
2 tablespoons pine nuts (activated
  if possible*), toasted
2 tablespoons lemon juice
125 ml (½ cup) extra-virgin olive oil

* See Glossary

Preheat the oven to 220°C (200°C fan-forced).

Place the zucchini in a large roasting tin and toss with the oil or fat. Season with salt and pepper, then spread the zucchini rounds out to form a single layer, making sure they're not bunched up. Roast for 12–15 minutes, or until the zucchini is tender and golden.

Meanwhile, place all the pesto ingredients in a mortar or the bowl of a food processor and pound with a pestle or process to form a thick, coarse paste. Taste and season with salt and pepper.

Transfer the roast zucchini to a serving bowl, add the spinach, pickled red onion and pesto and gently toss to coat. Serve immediately.

Serves 4–6

Pumpkin soup will always be a family favourite, as it ticks all the boxes when it comes to flavour. It is also budget friendly, very easy to get on the table and a great time saver; you can make up a big batch and freeze the leftovers to have on hand for when you need a quick meal. With this recipe I have lightly spiced it with curry powder and added cashews for a lovely texture. If you wanted to add some fish or prawns, then be my guest.

SPICED PUMPKIN AND CASHEW SOUP

2 tablespoons coconut oil or
    good-quality animal fat,* melted
1 onion, chopped
2 celery stalks, chopped
2 carrots, cut into 1.5 cm dice
4 garlic cloves, finely chopped
1½ tablespoons finely grated ginger
1½ teaspoons ground turmeric
1 teaspoon ground cumin
¼ teaspoon ground cinnamon
120 g cashew nuts (activated if possible*)
1 litre vegetable stock or
    Chicken Bone Broth (page 312)
500 g butternut pumpkin, cut into
    2 cm dice
2 tomatoes, cut into 2 cm dice
400 ml coconut milk
sea salt and freshly ground
    black pepper
2 handfuls of baby spinach leaves

To serve
roughly chopped coriander leaves
a couple of pinches of chilli flakes
    (if you like it a little spicy)

* See Glossary

Heat the oil or fat in a large saucepan over medium heat. Add the onion, celery and carrot and cook, stirring occasionally, for 8 minutes, or until the veggies are softened and slightly caramelised. Add the garlic, ginger and spices and cook for 1 minute, or until fragrant. Stir in the cashews and stock or broth and bring to the boil. Reduce the heat to low, cover with a lid and simmer for 15 minutes.

Increase the heat to medium–low, add the pumpkin, tomato and coconut milk to the pan, stir and bring back to the boil. Simmer, uncovered, for 20 minutes, or until the veggies are tender. Season with salt and pepper and stir in the spinach. Ladle the soup into warm bowls, scatter on the coriander and chilli flakes (if using) and serve.

Serves 4 as a side

Roasting sweet potatoes brings out even more texture and flavour from this versatile vegetable. I love to pair it with some sort of flavoured mayo and warm things up with spiced seeds to give it extra crunch. You can serve these wedges alongside pretty well any type of animal protein, and they are a delicious snack or lunch-box inclusion for kids and adults.

SWEET POTATO WEDGES WITH SMOKED PAPRIKA AIOLI

3 sweet potatoes (about 1 kg),
    cut into wedges
3 tablespoons melted coconut oil

Seed seasoning
1 tablespoon sesame seeds
1 tablespoon coriander seeds
1 tablespoon fennel seeds
1 tablespoon pumpkin seeds
    (activated if possible*)
1 teaspoon chilli flakes (optional)
2 teaspoons sea salt

Smoked paprika aioli
200 g Aioli (page 310)
1 teaspoon smoked paprika,
    plus extra for dusting

* See Glossary

Preheat the oven to 220°C (200°C fan-forced). Line a large baking tray with baking paper.

Place the sweet potato in a large bowl, add the coconut oil and toss to coat the wedges. Arrange the wedges on the prepared tray in a single layer and roast, rotating the tray halfway through, for 40–50 minutes, or until cooked and golden.

Meanwhile, to make the seed seasoning, place a large frying pan over medium heat. Add the sesame, coriander, fennel and pumpkin seeds and toast, tossing and stirring frequently, for 1 minute, or until lightly golden and fragrant. Transfer the seeds to a spice grinder, add the chilli flakes (if using) and grind to a coarse powder. Alternatively, use a mortar and pestle to do this. Tip into a small bowl, mix in the salt and set aside.

To make the smoked paprika aioli, combine the ingredients in another bowl and mix well. Dust the top with a little extra smoked paprika.

Sprinkle the seed seasoning and some extra smoked paprika over the sweet potato wedges and serve with the smoked paprika aioli on the side for dipping.

Serves 4–6 as a side

One thing I have learned in all my time cooking, especially after judging *My Kitchen Rules* for more than ten years, is that everyone has a different palate. Take this dish, for instance, which I've nicknamed 'cooked-to-death vegetables'. Some people absolutely love their veggies to be very well cooked; others like crisp just-cooked or raw veggies. Whatever you prefer will do just fine, as all I want to promote is eating more vegetables! This one is perfect served with grilled fish and mayo.

OVERCOOKED VEGGIES WITH GARLIC AND CHILLI

300 g green cabbage, roughly chopped
4 celery stalks, halved lengthways, then cut into 8 cm batons
2 zucchini, cut on an angle into 2 cm thick slices
5 silverbeet leaves, trimmed and roughly chopped into 10 cm lengths
½ large head of broccoli (about 200 g), cut into florets
150 g green beans, trimmed and halved
125 ml (½ cup) melted coconut oil or good-quality animal fat*
800 ml Chicken Bone Broth (page 312), vegetable stock or water, plus extra if needed
1 bunch of English spinach, trimmed and roughly chopped
sea salt and freshly ground black pepper
8 garlic cloves, finely chopped
2 long red chillies, halved, deseeded and finely chopped

Preheat the oven to 170°C (150°C fan-forced).

Evenly scatter the cabbage, celery, zucchini, silverbeet, broccoli and beans in a large roasting tin, add 3 tablespoons of oil or fat and toss to coat. Pour in the broth, stock or water. Cover with a lid or a baking tray and roast, stirring the veggies from time to time, for 45 minutes.

Increase the temperature to 200°C (180°C fan-forced). Remove the lid and roast the veggies for a further 30 minutes, making sure you stir them from time to time to prevent burning. Add the spinach, mix with the veggies and pour in more liquid if needed. Return, uncovered, to the oven for a further 15 minutes, or until the veggies are cooked through and slightly golden and the spinach is wilted. Season with salt and pepper.

Meanwhile, heat the remaining oil or fat in a frying pan over medium heat. Add the garlic and chilli and cook for 1–1½ minutes, or until lightly golden and fragrant.

Pour the garlic and chilli oil over the veggies and serve.

Serves 6–8 as a side

Seeing as every single page of this book is a celebration of vegetables, the art of roasting large vegetables needed to feature. With a gorgeous butternut pumpkin, it is as easy as cutting it in half, then roasting the halves with a delicious Moroccan spice mix and serving them with herbs and a spicy aioli, as we have done here. Or you can roast them whole then cut open and season afterwards. Serve alongside your favourite roast meat.

ROASTED BUTTERNUT PUMPKIN WITH SUMAC AIOLI

1 butternut pumpkin (about 1.8–2 kg), halved lengthways and deseeded
2 tablespoons coconut oil or good-quality animal fat,* melted
3 teaspoons ras el hanout* or ground cumin
sea salt and freshly ground black pepper
1 handful of pumpkin seeds (activated if possible*)
1 small handful of mint sprigs, some leaves picked

Sumac aioli
½ teaspoon sumac,* plus a couple of extra pinches to serve
200 g Aioli (page 310)

* See Glossary

Preheat the oven to 180°C (160°C fan-forced).

Brush the pumpkin with the oil or fat. Place in a roasting tin, cut-side up, sprinkle on the ras el hanout or cumin and season with salt and pepper. Roast for 1¼–1½ hours, or until tender.

Meanwhile, to make the sumac aioli, combine the sumac and aioli in a bowl.

Carefully transfer the roasted pumpkin to a large platter. Spoon over the sumac aioli, sprinkle on the pumpkin seeds and extra sumac and scatter over the mint.

Bread

Macadamia Fat Bomb Bread/
Charcoal Bread/ Paleo Flatbreads/
Nic's Amazing Hemp Bread/
Spiced Pumpkin Bread/ Savoury
Zucchini Bread/ Chocolate
and Beetroot Bread

Makes 1 × 20 cm loaf
(10–12 slices)

Sara Karan, a cancer survivor who featured in my documentary *The Magic Pill*, has kindly agreed to share her much-requested recipe for macadamia fat bomb bread – and here it is in all its glory. Thanks, Sarah!

MACADAMIA FAT BOMB BREAD

225 g macadamia nuts
    (activated if possible*)
140 g almond butter
    (or other nut butter)
80 ml (⅓ cup) melted coconut oil
½ teaspoon fine sea salt
2 tablespoons apple cider vinegar
6 eggs
2 teaspoons baking powder

To serve
extra-virgin olive oil
balsamic vinegar
dukkah

* See Glossary

Preheat the oven to 180°C (160°C fan-forced). Grease a 20 cm × 10 cm loaf tin and line the base and sides with baking paper, cutting into the corners to fit.

Blitz the macadamia nuts in a high-speed blender or food processor for about 6 minutes, or until a paste forms. Add the almond butter, coconut oil, salt and vinegar and blend, scraping down the side from time to time, to a wet paste. Add the eggs and baking powder and blend to combine.

Scoop the mixture into the prepared tin and spread out evenly. Bake for 1 hour, rotating the tin halfway through so the loaf cooks evenly. To check if the bread is cooked, insert a skewer in the centre; if it comes out clean, it's ready. Allow to cool a little in the tin, then turn out onto a wire rack to cool completely.

Thinly slice the bread and eat with whatever tickles your fancy. We love to dip this bread in olive oil, balsamic vinegar and homemade dukkah.

Store the bread in an airtight container in the fridge for up to 5 days or sliced in the freezer for up to 3 months.

Makes 1 × 20 cm loaf
(10–12 slices)

Charcoal bread has become quite trendy, with interpretations from loaves to bao (steamed buns) appearing on restaurant and cafe menus everywhere. Here is a version we make at home from time to time. You can add so many different spreads and toppings to this bread that you will never ever get bored with the breakfasts, school or work lunches, canapés and dinners you can create using it. For a stunning contrast, why not make delicious crispy croutons to sprinkle over a salad or some pumpkin soup?

CHARCOAL BREAD

70 g psyllium husks*
70 g (½ cup) coconut flour,
    plus extra for dusting
2 tablespoons hemp protein
    powder (see Note)
60 g (½ cup) sunflower seeds
2 tablespoons activated charcoal*
2 tablespoons chia seeds
1 tablespoon coconut sugar or honey
3 teaspoons baking powder
1½ teaspoons sea salt
1 tablespoon apple cider vinegar
3 eggs
2 tablespoons coconut oil, melted

* See Glossary

Preheat the oven to 180°C (160°C fan-forced). Grease a 20 cm × 10 cm loaf tin and line the base and sides with baking paper, cutting into the corners to fit.

Place the psyllium husks, coconut flour, hemp protein powder, sunflower seeds and activated charcoal in the bowl of a food processor and whiz for a few seconds until the seeds are finely chopped.

Transfer the flour mixture to a large bowl, then mix in the chia seeds, coconut sugar or honey, baking powder and salt.

In another bowl, combine the vinegar, eggs and 450 ml of water and whisk until smooth.

Add the coconut oil and the egg mixture to the dry ingredients and mix well to form a wet dough.

Knead the dough on a lightly floured work surface for 1 minute, then roll into a ball. Place in the prepared tin and pat down. Bake for 1½ hours, rotating the tin halfway through so the loaf cooks evenly. To check if it is cooked, remove the bread from the tin, then tap the base; if it sounds hollow, it's ready. If the loaf seems to be very heavy and dense, bake for a little longer. Allow to cool a little in the tin before turning out onto a wire rack to cool completely. Cut into thick slices to serve.

Store the charcoal bread in an airtight container in the fridge for up to 5 days or sliced in the freezer for up to 3 months.

Note
– You can buy hemp protein powder from health-food stores and online.

Makes 7

I love flatbreads. They are perfect to dunk in a delicious curry, dip, soup or braise, or to serve with some yummy topping, paleo 'cheese' or spread. Here is a grain-free version that won't cause any issues for your gut.

PALEO FLATBREADS

130 g (1⅓ cups) almond meal
130 g tapioca flour*
¼ teaspoon baking powder
125 ml (½ cup) coconut milk
1 egg
½ teaspoon sea salt
coconut oil or good-quality animal fat,* for cooking

* See Glossary

Combine the almond meal, tapioca flour, baking powder, coconut milk, egg and 125 ml (½ cup) of water in a bowl, season with salt and mix well.

Lightly oil a medium non-stick frying pan, place a sheet of baking paper in the pan and place the pan over medium heat. Add 3 tablespoons of batter to the pan and swirl around slightly. Cook for 3 minutes on one side, then flip, remove the paper and cook for 3 minutes, or until lightly golden. If the first side is still a bit pale, cook for another minute or so until golden. Place the flatbread on a plate and keep warm. Repeat with the remaining batter to make seven flatbreads.

Tip
– Store these flatbreads in an airtight container in the fridge for up to 1 week or freeze for up to 3 months.

CRISPY PALEO FLATBREADS WITH ZA'ATAR

7 x Paleo Flatbreads (see above)
olive oil, for brushing
za'atar,* for sprinkling
sea salt

* See Glossary

Preheat the oven to 200°C (180°C fan-forced). Line two large baking trays with baking paper.

Place the flatbreads on the prepared trays in a single layer. Brush each flatbread with about ½ teaspoon of olive oil and sprinkle each with about ½ teaspoon of za'atar.

Place in the oven and toast for 8–10 minutes, or until lightly golden and crisp. Keep a close eye on them, as they can burn quickly.

Makes 1 × 20 cm loaf
(10–12 slices)

I am very lucky to have my wife, Nic, by my side on this amazing journey of love and life. Nic's a whiz in the kitchen and uses intuition, not recipes, when it comes to cooking. My daughters and I always look forward to her creations. She has been making hemp bread for some time and, as Australia has now legalised hemp as a food source for humans, we can finally share her recipe. Thanks, Nic, for actually writing the recipe down. We love you! xoxo

NIC'S AMAZING HEMP BREAD

145 g (1 cup) hemp seeds (see Note)
170 g (1 cup) golden or brown flaxseeds
250 ml (1 cup) hot water
40 g (½ cup) psyllium husks*
3 tablespoons coconut flour,
 plus extra for dusting
8 eggs
1 tablespoon apple cider vinegar
1 teaspoon sesame oil
1 teaspoon bicarbonate of soda
1½ teaspoons fine sea salt

* See Glossary

Place the hemp seeds and flaxseeds in a bowl, pour in the hot water and stir well. Allow to soak for 1 hour at room temperature (the seeds will expand and absorb the water).

Preheat the oven to 170°C (150°C fan-forced). Grease a 20 cm × 10 cm loaf tin and line the base and sides with baking paper, cutting into the corners to fit.

Transfer the soaked seed mixture to the bowl of a food processor and process for 2 minutes, scraping down the side regularly to ensure the mix blends evenly, until a wet dough forms. Next, add the psyllium husks and coconut flour and blend until well combined. Add the eggs, vinegar, sesame oil, bicarbonate of soda and salt and blend for about 1 minute to form a thick dough.

Place the dough in the prepared tin and pat down. Bake for 1½ hours, rotating the tin halfway through so the loaf cooks evenly. To check if the bread is cooked, insert a skewer in the centre; if it comes out clean, it's ready. Allow the bread to cool a little in the tin before turning out onto a wire rack to cool completely. Cut into thick slices to serve.

Store in an airtight container in the fridge for up to 5 days or sliced in the freezer for up to 3 months.

Note
– You can purchase hemp seeds from health-food stores and online.

Makes 1 × 20 cm loaf
(10–12 slices)

Pumpkin is one of my top five vegetables and this year, for the first time, I grew my own. Boy, was I thrilled! Pumpkin is incredibly versatile and lends itself to so many recipes and creations: try it in soups, curries and stir-fries; add it to roasts, salads, breakfast dishes and hummus; and use it to whip up desserts or fry up pumpkin chips. This delightful pumpkin bread makes sensational sandwiches and fantastic French toast or try it slathered with something sweet – you really can't go wrong.

SPICED PUMPKIN BREAD

8 eggs
1 tablespoon apple cider vinegar
1 teaspoon sea salt
½ teaspoon garlic powder
¼ teaspoon freshly grated nutmeg
½ teaspoon ground ginger
¼ teaspoon freshly ground
　black pepper
80 ml (⅓ cup) olive oil
1 tablespoon coconut flour
100 g (1 cup) almond meal
3 tablespoons psyllium husks*
1 tablespoon baking powder
400 g Pumpkin Puree (page 322)
2 tablespoons pumpkin seeds
　(activated if possible*)
1 teaspoon nutritional yeast flakes*
　(optional)

* See Glossary

Preheat the oven to 160°C (140°C fan-forced). Grease a 20 cm × 10 cm loaf tin and line the base and sides with baking paper, cutting into the corners to fit.

Using a whisk, combine the eggs, vinegar, salt, garlic powder, nutmeg, ginger, pepper and olive oil in a large bowl. Add the coconut flour, almond meal, psyllium husks and baking powder and mix well. Gently swirl in the pumpkin puree.

Spoon the dough into the prepared tin, spread out evenly and sprinkle on the pumpkin seeds and nutritional yeast (if using). Bake for 1½ hours, rotating the tin halfway through so the loaf cooks evenly. To check if the bread is cooked, insert a skewer in the centre; if it comes out clean, it's ready. Remove from the oven and allow to cool a little in the tin before turning out onto a wire rack to cool completely. Cut the bread into thick slices to serve.

Store in an airtight container in the fridge for up to 5 days or sliced in the freezer for up to 3 months.

Makes 1 × 20 cm loaf
(10–12 slices)

With an abundance of zucchini coming out of my veggie garden in the summer months, I like to find lots of creative ways to use them. Eat them straight up in salads, use your spiraliser to make noodles, add them to chilled or warm soups, sauces or roasts, or whip up this bread – it's great for a delicious lunch or after-school snack, with your favourite sandwich fillings or sweet or savoury spread.

SAVOURY ZUCCHINI BREAD

160 g almond meal
40 g coconut flour
2 tablespoons psyllium husks*
2 teaspoons baking powder
1 teaspoon sea salt
450 g grated zucchini
3 garlic cloves, finely grated
1½ teaspoons finely chopped rosemary
6 eggs, lightly beaten
120 ml extra-virgin olive oil
Paleo Butter (page 320), to serve
   (optional)

* See Glossary

Preheat the oven to 160°C (140°C fan-forced). Grease a 20 cm × 10 cm loaf tin and line the base and sides with baking paper, cutting into the corners to fit.

Combine the almond meal, coconut flour, psyllium husks, baking powder and salt in a large bowl. Add the zucchini, garlic, rosemary, eggs and olive oil and stir well.

Spoon the zucchini mixture into the prepared tin and spread out evenly. Bake for 1½ hours, rotating the tin halfway through so the loaf cooks evenly. To check if the bread is cooked, insert a skewer in the centre; if it comes out clean, it's ready. Allow to cool a little in the tin before turning out onto a wire rack to cool completely. Cut into thick slices and serve with some paleo butter, if you like.

Store in an airtight container in the fridge for up to 5 days or sliced in the freezer for up to 3 months.

Makes 1 × 20 cm loaf
(10–12 slices)

Beetroot has a natural sweetness and its wonderful colour permeates any recipe it is used in. Fascinatingly, it works well with chocolate. I feel certain this delicious bread will become one of your favourite treats.

CHOCOLATE AND BEETROOT BREAD

70 g (½ cup) coconut flour
80 g (¾ cup) almond meal
1 teaspoon ground cinnamon
2 teaspoons bicarbonate of soda
pinch of sea salt
6 eggs
¼ teaspoon vanilla powder or paste
130 g honey, plus extra for brushing
250 g grated beetroot
250 ml (1 cup) melted coconut oil,
    plus extra to serve (optional)
300 g dark (70–90% cacao) chocolate,
    chopped, plus extra finely grated
    to serve
almond butter, to serve (optional)

Preheat the oven to 160°C (140°C fan-forced). Grease a 20 cm × 10 cm loaf tin and line the base and sides with baking paper, cutting into the corners to fit.

In a large bowl, combine the coconut flour, almond meal, cinnamon, bicarbonate of soda and salt and mix well.

In another bowl, whisk together the eggs, vanilla and honey, then stir in the beetroot.

Pour the liquid ingredients into the dry ingredients and stir with a wooden spoon until thoroughly combined. Add the coconut oil and 250 g of the chopped chocolate and stir until incorporated.

Spoon the dough into the prepared tin and spread out evenly with a spatula. Bake for 1 hour and 10 minutes, rotating the tin halfway through so the loaf cooks evenly. Cover the loaf with baking paper if it starts to get too dark. To check if the bread is cooked, insert a skewer in the centre; if it comes out clean, it's ready. Cool in the tin for 5 minutes, then carefully turn out onto a wire rack to cool completely.

Meanwhile, melt the remaining chopped chocolate in a heatproof bowl over a saucepan of just-simmering water. (Make sure the bowl doesn't touch the water or it will overheat and the chocolate will seize.)

Brush the melted chocolate over the top of the bread and cool for 10 minutes. Sprinkle the grated chocolate over the top. Slice and serve toasted, spread with some coconut oil or almond butter, if desired.

Snacks

Roasted Carrot Hummus with Raw Veggies/ Smoked Paprika Cauliflower Popcorn/ Pumpkin 'Cheese' with Savoury Crackers/ Cauliflower Hummus with Toasted Seeds/ Old-Fashioned Chow Chow Relish/ Salt and Vinegar Sweet Potato Crisps/ Paleo Piccalilli/ Toasted Coconut Chutney/ Beetroot 'Cheese'/ Pickled Curried Eggplant/ Baba Ghanoush/ Veganmite/ Zucchini 'Cheese'/ Onion Rings with Chipotle Aioli/ Smashed Avo and Salad Sandwich/ Pumpkin and Chilli Chocolate Mousse

Serves 4

This dish is awesome ... and so simple to prepare. You can make up a big batch of the hummus and freeze it in portions, then when friends drop in, pull it out and serve it with an array of in-season organic vegetables and seed crackers. This also makes a great snack to add to the kids' lunch boxes or to use as a base for some grilled fish.

ROASTED CARROT HUMMUS WITH RAW VEGGIES

2 tablespoons coconut oil, melted, plus extra for greasing
600 g carrots, cut into 2.5 cm pieces
½ teaspoon ground cumin
sea salt and freshly ground black pepper
4 Garlic Confit cloves (page 318) or roasted garlic cloves
90 g hulled tahini
1 teaspoon finely grated ginger
3 tablespoons lemon juice
80 ml (⅓ cup) extra-virgin olive oil, plus extra to serve

To serve
toasted sesame seeds
raw vegetables (such as carrot, capsicum, broccoli, fennel, celery, cucumber, radish, okra, cauliflower), cut into bite-sized pieces

Preheat the oven to 190°C (170°C fan-forced). Grease a large casserole dish with coconut oil.

Place the carrot in a single layer in the prepared casserole dish. Sprinkle on the cumin, salt and pepper and drizzle over the coconut oil. Mix with your hands to coat well, then roast for 20 minutes, or until the carrot is nicely coloured. Pour in 300 ml of water, cover with a lid and roast for a further 35–40 minutes, or until the carrot is very tender. Allow to cool.

Place the carrot and all the cooking juices in the bowl of a food processor and process until smooth. Add the garlic, tahini, ginger, lemon juice and olive oil and whiz until smooth. Add a little water if needed. Season with salt and pepper.

Spoon the carrot hummus into a serving bowl, drizzle on some extra olive oil and sprinkle over the sesame seeds. Serve with the raw vegetables on the side.

The carrot hummus will keep in an airtight container in the fridge for up to 5 days.

Serves 4

How cool is it that we live in a time where we are not bound by cultural history and can create new and wonderful recipes that celebrate vegetables? Take this simple but very addictive snack of cauliflower popcorn. It sounds quite bizarre but in actual fact is so simple you will wonder why this has never become a classic – until now! Make me proud and add this to your cooking repertoire.

SMOKED PAPRIKA CAULIFLOWER POPCORN

2 ½ tablespoons coconut oil, melted
1 tablespoon smoked paprika
sea salt
1 head of cauliflower (about 1 kg),
    cut into bite-sized florets
Mayonnaise (page 320) or Aioli
    (page 310), to serve (optional)

Preheat the oven to 200°C (180°C fan-forced). Line two baking trays with baking paper.

Place the oil, paprika and ½ teaspoon of salt in a large bowl and mix to combine. Add the cauliflower and toss to coat thoroughly.

Spread the cauliflower in a single layer on the prepared trays. Roast for 20–25 minutes, stirring and turning the cauliflower halfway through, until golden.

Sprinkle with a little more salt, if desired, and serve with some mayonnaise or aioli for dipping, if you like.

Serves 6–8

When it comes to snacks, I am a bit of a cheese-and-crackers type of guy. Here is a little pumpkin 'cheese' and crackers number that is fun, delicious and nutritionally superior. It will get your guests talking and smiling as they devour it.

PUMPKIN 'CHEESE' WITH SAVOURY CRACKERS

120 g cashew nuts
400 g Pumpkin Puree (page 322)
60 g powdered gelatine*
150 ml hot water
3 tablespoons nutritional yeast flakes*
2 tablespoons coconut oil,
    plus extra for greasing
1 tablespoon lemon juice, or to taste
sea salt and freshly ground
    black pepper

Savoury crackers
200 g (2 cups) almond meal
1 large egg
2 tablespoons coconut oil or
    good-quality animal fat,* melted
tapioca flour, * for dusting

To serve
a few sage leaves (optional)
gherkins

* See Glossary

Soak the cashews in 500 ml (2 cups) of cold water for at least 6 hours. Drain and rinse well.

Place the pumpkin puree, soaked cashews, gelatine, water, nutritional yeast, oil and lemon juice in a blender, add 1 teaspoon of salt and blend for 30 seconds, or until very smooth. Taste and add more salt and lemon juice if needed.

Lightly grease a large ramekin or a 15 cm round cake tin, then pour in the pumpkin mixture. Cover and refrigerate for 2 hours, or until set.

Meanwhile, preheat the oven to 170°C (150°C fan-forced). Line a baking tray with baking paper.

To make the savoury crackers, place the almond meal, egg, oil or fat and ½ teaspoon each of salt and pepper in the bowl of a food processor and process to combine. Turn the mixture out onto a lightly floured (with tapioca) bench and knead to form a dough. Place the dough between two sheets of baking paper and roll out to 3 mm thick. Prick the dough with a fork, then cut into rectangles, squares or rounds using a knife or cookie cutter. Sprinkle with a little extra salt and pepper, if desired, and place on the prepared tray. Bake for 15 minutes, or until lightly golden. Allow to cool on the tray before serving.

Turn out the pumpkin 'cheese' onto a platter, scatter over the sage leaves (if using) and sprinkle some pepper over the top. Serve with the savoury crackers and gherkins.

Serves 4–6

This is an excellent snack to whip up for family and friends when cauliflowers are cheap and abundant. The toasted spiced seeds and crispy paleo flatbreads provide the perfect crunchy contrast to the creamy hummus.

CAULIFLOWER HUMMUS WITH TOASTED SEEDS

½ head of cauliflower
(about 500 g), cut into florets
4 garlic cloves, peeled
80 ml (⅓ cup) olive oil
½ teaspoon sea salt
¾ teaspoon ground cumin
2 ½ tablespoons lemon juice,
or to taste
2 tablespoons hulled tahini

To serve
extra-virgin olive oil
Toasted Spiced Seeds (page 323)
Crispy Paleo Flatbreads with
Za'atar (page 250)

Place a steamer basket over a saucepan of boiling water. Add the cauliflower and garlic cloves and steam for 20–25 minutes, or until the cauliflower is very tender. Remove the cauliflower and garlic and allow to cool completely in a colander.

Place the cauliflower, garlic and the remaining ingredients in a high-speed blender and blend until smooth. Adjust the seasoning with a little more salt if needed.

Place the cauliflower hummus in a serving bowl, drizzle over the extra-virgin olive oil and sprinkle on the toasted spiced seeds. Serve with the flatbreads.

Makes 2 × 1 litre jars

I wanted to share this recipe with you as it highlights vegetables at their peak. Chow chow is a classic American relish. The main ingredients are generally green or red tomatoes and capsicums. Having said that, some recipes (like this one) call for cabbage too. So, when you have a surplus of tomatoes, capsicum and/or cabbage and don't know what to do with them, chow chow will come to the rescue. This works extremely well with eggs, hotdogs and seafood dishes, like old-school fish cakes.

OLD-FASHIONED CHOW CHOW RELISH

300 ml apple cider vinegar
260 g (¾ cup) honey
1 tablespoon sea salt
1 teaspoon mustard powder
2 teaspoons mustard seeds
½ teaspoon chilli flakes
    (add more if you like it spicy!)
½ teaspoon celery seeds
¾ teaspoon ground turmeric
½ teaspoon ground ginger
1 green capsicum, cut into 2 cm dice
1 red capsicum, cut into 2 cm dice
4 green tomatoes, cut into 2 cm dice
2 red onions, cut into 2 cm dice
150 g (1½ cups) diced green cabbage

You'll need two 1 litre preserving jars with screw-top lids for this recipe. Wash the jars and all utensils you will be using in very hot water or run them through a hot rinse cycle in the dishwasher.

Combine the vinegar, honey, salt, spices and 3 tablespoons of water in a large saucepan over medium–high heat and bring to the boil.

Reduce the heat to medium–low. Add all the vegetables to the pan, then stir and continue to cook for 15–18 minutes, or until the vegetables are tender crisp. Fill the prepared jars while still hot, making sure the veggies are submerged in the liquid. Screw on the lid and leave to cool on the benchtop (this helps to vacuum seal the jars), then pop in the fridge. Allow the flavours to develop for at least 1 day before eating. For best results, leave for 4 days. Once opened, this relish will keep for up to 3 weeks in the fridge. Unopened, it will keep for 2 months in the fridge.

Tip
– Any leftover pickling juice can be used for dressings.

Serves 4

If you ever want to see the kids eat veggies without a second thought, look no further than the addictive and super yummy sweet potato crisp. We have been making these for years and they come in handy as an after-school or weekend treat for the kids and their friends – and adults love them as well. For this version, I have teamed the crisps with two favourite ingredients that work hand in hand: salt and vinegar. If you make a big batch you can top them with chicken liver parfait or guacamole, or make some paleo nachos with them.

SALT AND VINEGAR SWEET POTATO CRISPS

400 ml melted coconut oil or
    good-quality animal fat*
2 sweet potatoes (about 500 g),
    thinly sliced with a mandoline
    or sharp knife

Vinegar salt
100 ml apple cider vinegar
    or white wine vinegar
80 g sea salt flakes

* See Glossary

Preheat the oven to 180°C (160°C fan-forced). Line a baking tray with baking paper.

To make the vinegar salt, place the vinegar and salt in a small bowl and mix to combine, then spread out on the prepared tray and bake for 12–15 minutes, or until crisp and dry. When cool enough to handle, crumble into flakes and set aside until needed.

Heat the oil or fat in a large saucepan over medium–high heat until the temperature reaches about 160°C. (To test, drop a sweet potato slice into the hot oil; if it starts bubbling straight away, it is ready.) Fry the sliced sweet potato in batches for 2–3½ minutes, or until just starting to colour. Keep a close eye on the sweet potato at all times, as the crisps can burn very quickly. Remove with a slotted spoon and drain on paper towel. Season with the vinegar salt and serve at once.

The crisps can be stored in an airtight container for up to 3 days.

Tips
– Store the leftover vinegar salt in an airtight container in the pantry for up to 3 months.
– The leftover oil or fat can be reused as cooking oil for other recipes. Store in an airtight jar in the fridge for up to 3 weeks.

Makes 2 × 1 litre jars

Piccalilli, an English version of Indian spiced pickles, is mainly used as a condiment to serve alongside charcuterie or small goods like ham, terrines, sausages, bacon, burgers and hotdogs. It also works well with fish, eggs and vegetables. This is one of those condiments that you will end up making time and time again, as it is super simple and immensely satisfying, and gives your meals that little bit extra.

PALEO PICCALILLI

2 small zucchini (about 400 g)
½ small head of cauliflower
   (about 400 g)
200 g green beans
4 pickling onions
80 g sea salt
6 garlic cloves, peeled and halved
500 ml (2 cups) apple cider vinegar
200 g honey
2 teaspoons cumin seeds, crushed
2 teaspoons coriander seeds, crushed
3 teaspoons yellow mustard seeds
1 tablespoon mustard powder
1 tablespoon ground turmeric
2 tablespoons tapioca flour* mixed
   with 3 tablespoons cold water
2 large cabbage leaves, washed

* See Glossary

You will need two 1 litre preserving jars with airlock lids for this recipe. Wash the jars and all utensils you will be using in very hot water or run them through a hot rinse cycle in the dishwasher.

Trim and cut all the vegetables into bite-sized pieces.

In a bowl large enough to fit all the veggies and 1.5 litres of water, pour in the water, add the salt and stir until dissolved, then mix in the veggies and garlic. Put a plate on top to keep the veggies submerged in the liquid, then cover and place in the fridge for 24 hours.

The next day, drain the veggies and rinse well with cold running water.

Place the vinegar, honey, spices, tapioca mixture and 200 ml of water in a large saucepan over medium heat, stir well and simmer for 5 minutes, or until the liquid thickens. Stir in the veggies and cook for a further 5 minutes, or until the veggies are slightly soft. Allow to cool, then transfer to the prepared jars.

Take the cabbage leaves, fold them up and place one on top of the cauliflower mixture in each jar, then add a small glass weight (a shot glass is ideal) to keep everything submerged. Close the lid and wrap a tea towel around each jar to block out the light. Leave in a dark, cool place for at least 1 week. For best results, allow to pickle for 2 weeks.

Once opened, store the piccalilli in the fridge for up to 4 weeks. Unopened, it will keep for up to 3 months in the fridge.

Makes 280 g

This is one of the most brilliant recipes in this book, and it needs to be experienced to be truly understood. We have amazing flavour profiles with the sweetness of dried fruit, the melody of spices and the rich fattiness of coconut. Be prepared for the texture adventure that happens in your mouth: crunchiness, chewiness and an overall brilliant mouthfeel. Delicious served with any curry, this also works on eggs, salads, soups, seafood, meat and any vegetable dish that needs a bit of a lift.

TOASTED COCONUT CHUTNEY

1 tablespoon coriander seeds
55 g (1 cup) coconut flakes, lightly toasted and roughly chopped
155 g (1 cup) cashew nuts, lightly toasted and finely chopped
3 tablespoons golden raisins, chopped
3 tablespoons white sesame seeds, toasted
½ teaspoon chilli flakes, or to taste
¼ teaspoon ground cumin
½ teaspoon sea salt
¼ teaspoon freshly ground black pepper

Place the coriander seeds in a small frying pan over medium heat and toast, shaking the pan occasionally, for 1 minute, or until fragrant and light brown. Remove and grind in a spice grinder or using a mortar and pestle.

Combine all the ingredients in a bowl and mix well. Transfer to a glass storage jar, seal and store in a cool, dark place for up to 1 month.

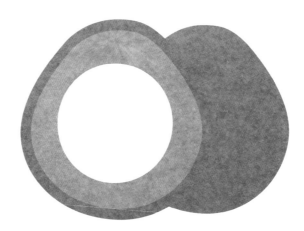

Serves 6–8

Beetroot are one of the most nutritious foods on the planet with high levels of vitamin C, which is anti-inflammatory and helps lower blood pressure. When they are in season I like to include them in my diet at least once a week. This showstopper of a dish is the perfect way to encourage your family and guests to eat more beetroot. I love to serve this as part of a platter with olives, sliced meat, cold cooked prawns, pickles and bread or crackers. You can also make individual portions in a muffin tin and freeze leftovers for a later date.

BEETROOT 'CHEESE'

500 g beetroot, grated
60 g powdered gelatine*
2 tablespoons olive oil or
    melted coconut oil
2½ tablespoons lemon juice, or to taste
1½ teaspoons sea salt, or to taste
2 tablespoons nutritional yeast flakes*
    (optional)
5 basil leaves, torn

To serve
finely grated horseradish
1 handful of watercress sprigs
olive oil, for drizzling
savoury crackers

* See Glossary

Line the base and sides of a 20 cm × 10 cm loaf tin with baking paper, cutting into the corners to fit.

Place the beetroot and 250 ml (1 cup) of water in a saucepan, cover with a lid and simmer, stirring occasionally, over medium heat for 15 minutes, or until the beetroot is cooked.

Place the beetroot and the liquid (you should have about 200 ml – if not, add some hot water) in a blender and blend until smooth. Pass through a fine sieve, discarding the leftover pulp. Pour the beetroot puree back into the blender, add the gelatine, oil, lemon juice, salt and nutritional yeast and blend for 30 seconds, or until very smooth. Add the basil and pulse once or twice just to mix through.

Immediately pour the beetroot mixture into the prepared tin, cover and refrigerate for 2 hours, or until set.

Turn out the beetroot 'cheese' onto a platter, then sprinkle on the grated horseradish and watercress and drizzle on the olive oil. Serve with some savoury crackers and enjoy.

Makes 1.4 kg

It is amazing how a simple accompaniment that can be made in bulk and stored for months can turn any old breakfast, lunch, dinner or snack into something special. Try this pickled eggplant number with your fried eggs and greens in the morning, or grill a fillet of fish, add a green salad or some sautéed spinach and serve alongside, or perhaps make a vegetable curry and some coconut yoghurt raita and pop this and some grilled paleo flatbreads (page 250) on the side.

PICKLED CURRIED EGGPLANT

2 large eggplants (about 1.15 kg
   in total), cut into 3 cm dice
2½ tablespoons sea salt
130 ml melted coconut oil
1 teaspoon yellow mustard seeds
5 garlic cloves, finely chopped
1 tablespoon finely grated ginger
2 long red chillies, halved on an angle
15 fresh curry leaves
1½ tablespoons curry powder
1 teaspoon ground turmeric
250 ml (1 cup) apple cider vinegar
70 g honey

You will need three 500 ml (2 cup) preserving jars for this recipe. Wash the jars and all utensils you will be using in very hot water or run them through a hot rinse cycle in the dishwasher.

Place the eggplant and 2 tablespoons of salt in a large bowl and toss well. Transfer to a colander and set aside for 30 minutes to allow the bitter juices to drain from the eggplant. Rinse the eggplant and pat dry with paper towel.

Heat the oil in a large saucepan over medium heat. Add the mustard seeds and cook for 20–30 seconds, or until just starting to pop. Add the garlic and ginger and cook, stirring, for a further 15 seconds, or until fragrant. Next, add the chilli, curry leaves, eggplant, curry powder and turmeric and cook, stirring frequently, for 6–8 minutes, or until the eggplant is half cooked. Stir in the vinegar, honey, remaining salt and 3 tablespoons of water and bring to the boil. Reduce the heat to medium–low and cook, stirring occasionally, for a further 8 minutes, or until the eggplant is tender. Remove from the heat.

While still hot, transfer the eggplant mixture to the prepared jars and tightly seal. Allow to stand until cool, then refrigerate.

Chill before eating. Once opened, it will keep for up to 3 weeks in the fridge. Unopened, it will keep for up to 3 months in the fridge.

Serves 4

Lately baba ghanoush has become a favourite dish to have on hand at home, which is funny, really, as I learned to make this about 30 years ago! I have come to love it on its own or as an addition to a meal. You can serve it the way we have done here, with some bread or crackers, or use it as a base for fried eggs, grilled fish or roasted meat. Add some fresh herbs, maybe a little dried fruit, preserved lemon and some pistachios and you are in for a real treat.

BABA GHANOUSH

1 large eggplant (about 500 g)
1½ tablespoons olive oil,
    plus extra to serve
50 g hulled tahini
2 Garlic Confit cloves (page 318)
1 tablespoon lemon juice,
    or more to taste
½ teaspoon ground cumin
⅛ teaspoon chilli powder
sea salt and freshly ground
    black pepper

To serve
3 tablespoons Crispy Garlic (page 315)
¼ teaspoon smoked paprika
1 tablespoon chopped flat-leaf
    parsley leaves
4 x Coconut Flour Pita Breads
    (page 314)

Cook the eggplant over an open flame on a stovetop or barbecue, turning frequently until the skin is charred and blistered and the flesh feels soft when pressed with tongs – about 8–10 minutes.

Place the charred eggplant in a large bowl, cover tightly and set aside to cool.

Transfer the cooled eggplant to a colander to drain the juice, then peel and discard the skin. Place the cooked eggplant flesh in the bowl of a food processor, add the olive oil, tahini, garlic, lemon juice, ground cumin and chilli powder and process until smooth. Season with salt and pepper. If the baba ghanoush is too thick, mix in a little cold water.

Spoon the baba ghanoush into a serving dish and drizzle over a little extra olive oil. Sprinkle with the crispy garlic, smoked paprika and chopped parsley and serve with the pita bread.

Makes 150 g

As a kid growing up in Australia, it was inevitable that Vegemite on toast would be a favourite snack to chow down on. Fast forward 30 years or so and I am pleased to share my take on Vegemite – a simple paleo spread that is so nutritious and full of flavour it will make your gut *and* tastebuds happy. Here, I suggest serving this on hemp bread but it also works wonders on macadamia, charcoal, seed, pumpkin or zucchini bread (see Bread chapter, page 245). If you are looking for a store-bought version, check out Cinnamon Morrissey's creation EveryMite – her story is one we should all support.

VEGANMITE

90 g (⅓ cup) black tahini
2 ½ tablespoons tamari or
     coconut aminos*
1 tablespoon nutritional yeast flakes*
¼ teaspoon garlic powder
¼ teaspoon onion powder
1 teaspoon apple cider vinegar

To serve
slices of Nic's Amazing Hemp Bread
     (page 252) or paleo bread
     of your choice
Paleo Butter (page 320), coconut
     oil or good-quality animal fat,*
     for spreading (optional)

* See Glossary

Place the tahini, tamari or coconut aminos, nutritional yeast, garlic and onion powders and vinegar in a high-speed blender and blend until smooth. Scoop out the paste and pop it straight into a glass jar.

To serve, toast the slices of bread, spread a thin layer of paleo butter, oil or fat on top, if desired, then spread on some veganmite and enjoy.

Store the veganmite in a sealed glass jar in the fridge for up to 4 weeks.

Serves 6–8

Here is a great cheese substitute that is perfect for those times when you want something to pop in school or work lunch boxes, or when you're really feeling like a cheese and cracker hit. Your tastebuds and gut will love it, especially as this zucchini 'cheese' includes good-quality gelatine, which is so good for our gut and overall health.

ZUCCHINI 'CHEESE'

500 g zucchini, cut into small dice
60 g powdered gelatine*
100 ml filtered hot water
2 tablespoons olive oil or melted coconut oil, plus extra olive oil to serve
2 tablespoons lemon juice, or to taste
1 teaspoon sea salt, or to taste
2 tablespoons nutritional yeast flakes*
1 small handful of basil leaves
freshly ground black pepper
mixed olives, to serve
sliced meats, to serve

* See Glossary

Line the base and sides of two 10 cm round tart tins or one 20 cm × 10 cm loaf tin with baking paper, cutting into the corners to fit.

Place the zucchini in a steamer basket over a saucepan of boiling water, cover and steam for about 8–10 minutes, or until very tender.

Transfer the zucchini to a blender, add the gelatine, hot water, oil, lemon juice, salt and nutritional yeast and blend for 30 seconds, or until very smooth.

Immediately pour the zucchini mixture into the prepared tin or tins, cover tightly and refrigerate for 2 hours, or until set.

Turn out the zucchini 'cheese' onto a platter. Scatter over a few basil leaves, drizzle with olive oil and finish with a grinding of black pepper. Slice and serve with some olives and sliced meats.

Serves 4–6

It was a few decades ago now that I was first, quite apprehensively, introduced to onion rings. Well, one bite later and I was hooked. Here, I've come up with a healthier yet still delicious version to share with you in all its sweet and crunchy glory. You don't really need a sauce to go with these, as the salt and vinegar are perfect, but if you'd like to add more wow factor, then why not try my chipotle aioli?

ONION RINGS WITH CHIPOTLE AIOLI

sea salt and freshly ground
  black pepper
coconut oil or good-quality animal
  fat,* for deep-frying
80 g tapioca flour,* for dusting
3 onions, cut into 1 cm thick
  rings, rings separated
Vinegar Salt (page 272)

Chipotle aioli
200 g Aioli (page 310)
1 teaspoon chipotle powder,
  or to taste

Kombucha batter
140 g tapioca flour
2 tablespoons coconut flour
¼ teaspoon bicarbonate of soda
160 ml kombucha
2 egg whites, beaten

* See Glossary

To make the chipotle aioli, place the aioli and chipotle powder in a small bowl and mix to combine. Set aside until needed.

To make the kombucha batter, place the tapioca and coconut flours and bicarbonate of soda in a bowl, season with salt and pepper and make a well in the centre. Add the kombucha and egg white, then whisk until smooth. Allow to stand for 10 minutes. Whisk again just before using.

Heat the oil to 180°C in a deep-fryer or large saucepan. (To test, drop a teaspoon of batter into the hot oil; if it starts bubbling straight away, it is ready.)

Season the tapioca flour with salt and pepper. Working in batches, lightly dust the onion rings with the tapioca flour, then dip in the kombucha batter, shaking off the excess. Carefully place in the hot oil and deep-fry, turning occasionally, for 2–3 minutes, or until golden. Drain on paper towel.

Sprinkle the vinegar salt on the fried onion rings and serve with the chipotle aioli for dipping.

Serves 2

There is something so nourishing about this recipe, with all its delicious and colourful veggies. I have incorporated some of my favourite sandwich fillings with a nut 'cheese', but you could easily leave that out or use some tahini or paleo hummus instead. Feel free to add roast chicken, beef, lamb or pork, or some tuna or salmon, if you are inclined.

SMASHED AVO AND SALAD SANDWICH

sea salt and freshly ground
   black pepper
4 sandwich-cut slices of your choice
   of paleo bread
1 Lebanese cucumber, sliced
½ baby cos lettuce, leaves separated
   and torn
1 tomato, sliced
1 small carrot, grated
100 g Macadamia 'Cheese' (page 320)

Smashed avo
1 avocado
2 teaspoons lemon juice

To make the smashed avo, mash the avocado with a fork until creamy but still slightly chunky. Add the lemon juice and mix until combined, then season with salt and pepper.

To assemble, spread the smashed avo on two slices of bread. Top each slice with half the cucumber, cos lettuce, tomato and carrot and season with salt and pepper. Spread the macadamia 'cheese' on the remaining slices of bread and then place, spread-side down, on top of the salad to form a sandwich. Cut the sandwiches in half and serve.

Serves 2–3

You may have noticed a recurring theme in this book – and I'm not talking about my love of vegetables. Something that generally flies under the radar is how the use of spices elevates dishes in terms of flavour and nutrients. Here, to add another dimension to an already stunning chocolate mousse, I have spiced things up with some heat. Feel free to go easy on or omit the chilli if serving this to kids; alternatively, use ground ginger instead. This dish is high in natural sugars, so please go easy as it is a treat.

PUMPKIN AND CHILLI CHOCOLATE MOUSSE

100 g dried or fresh medjool
    dates, pitted
150 g Pumpkin Puree (page 322)
1 avocado
40 g cacao powder
1 tablespoon honey
¼ teaspoon ground cinnamon
⅛ teaspoon vanilla powder
    or ¼ teaspoon vanilla paste
120 g Whipped Coconut Cream
    (page 323)
chilli powder or cayenne pepper,
    to serve

If using dried dates, place the dates in a small bowl and cover with warm water. Soak for 20 minutes to soften, then drain.

Place the dates, pumpkin puree, avocado flesh, cacao, honey, cinnamon and vanilla in the bowl of a food processor and process until very smooth and creamy. Fold through the coconut cream to combine.

Spoon the mousse into small bowls, sprinkle over the chilli powder or cayenne pepper and refrigerate for 30 minutes to set slightly before serving.

Ferments

Quick Kimchi/ Beetroot
Kvass/ Fermented Kohlrabi/
Cultured Cauliflower and
Celery/ Kitsa's Autumn Kraut/
Kick-Ass Turmeric Kimchi

Makes 1 × 1 litre jar

Real kimchi, a fermented cabbage and spice mixture, originates from Korea and is so loved that it is now a common fixture in many cafes and restaurants around the world. Nothing can beat the fermented version as it has gut-nourishing probiotics, but sometimes all you want is a quick side to a meal. If you are short on time and have some cabbage in the fridge, this nourishing and delicious recipe fits the bill perfectly.

QUICK KIMCHI

½ Chinese cabbage (wombok), cut into 5 cm pieces
2 tablespoons sea salt
4 garlic cloves, finely chopped
2 teaspoons finely grated ginger
1–2 tablespoons Korean chilli powder (gochugaru)* or chilli powder
2 tablespoons fish sauce
1½ tablespoons apple cider vinegar
1 tablespoon honey
3 spring onions, chopped
1 handful of coriander, roots, stalks and leaves, washed well and finely chopped
2 long red chillies, deseeded and thinly sliced
filtered water (optional)

* See Glossary

Combine the cabbage and salt in a large glass or stainless steel bowl and mix well. Cover and set aside for 1 hour to wilt the cabbage.

Meanwhile, place the garlic, ginger, chilli powder, fish sauce, vinegar and honey in a bowl and mix well. Set aside.

Rinse the cabbage thoroughly under cold water, drain well and pat dry. Transfer the cabbage to a large bowl, add the spring onion, coriander and chilli, then add the garlic and ginger mixture and toss well.

You can serve the kimchi straight away or, for better results, ferment it.

To ferment the kimchi, you'll need a 1 litre preserving jar with an airlock lid. Wash the jar and all utensils in very hot water or run them through a hot rinse cycle in the dishwasher.

Fill the prepared jar with the kimchi, pressing down well with a large spoon or potato masher to remove any air pockets. The vegetables should be completely submerged in the liquid; add some filtered water if necessary. Seal with the lid and ferment for 2–3 days in a cool, dark place. The longer you leave the kimchi to ferment the stronger the flavour will be. Chill before eating. Once opened, the kimchi will keep in the fridge for up to 3 weeks.

Serves 4

We enjoy a non-alcoholic fermented beverage every single day upon waking or just before a meal. The types of drink that we make and consume always vary, as they all have their own special properties; favourites include non-dairy kefir, kvass or kombucha. When we have beetroot on hand and leftover kraut juice from the jar we love to make kvass. It is so good for cultivating beneficial gut bacteria.

BEETROOT KVASS

2–4 beetroot (about 600 g)
1 tablespoon sea salt
250 ml (1 cup) filtered water, plus extra
½ sachet vegetable starter culture*
    or 3 tablespoons sauerkraut brine
    (to make your own sauerkraut,
    see page 322)

* See Glossary

You'll need a 1.5 litre preserving jar with an airlock lid for this recipe. Wash the jar and all utensils in very hot water or run them through a hot rinse cycle in the dishwasher.

Wash and scrub the beetroot (peel them if they are not organic), then chop into 1.5 cm cubes and place them in the jar.

Mix the salt, water and starter culture or sauerkraut brine in a glass measuring jug, then pour into the jar.

Fill the jar with filtered water, leaving 2 cm free at the top, and tightly secure the lid. Leave on the kitchen counter at room temperature for 4–7 days to ferment. Strain and chill before drinking.

The kvass will keep for 2 weeks in the fridge once opened.

Note
– Your kvass may develop a thin layer of white or brown foam on top during the fermentation process. This is harmless – simply scoop it out with a spoon before placing the kvass in the fridge to chill.

Makes 1 × 1.5 litre jar

Kohlrabi has become the darling of the restaurant world and is popping up on menus across the globe. Once you start to utilise this amazing ingredient in your cooking, I have no doubt you will fall in love with it too. Fermenting kohlrabi seems to be the method of choice for top chefs and lends itself to brightening up simple seafood dishes, as it adds a refreshing zinginess and texture.

FERMENTED KOHLRABI

3–4 kohlrabi, cut into 1.5 cm cubes
3 radishes, thinly sliced into rounds
½ teaspoon black peppercorns
1 bay leaf
¼ teaspoon caraway seeds
¼ teaspoon juniper seeds
¼ teaspoon mustard seeds
¼ teaspoon coriander seeds
5 cardamom pods (brown or green)
1½ teaspoons sea salt
   (or 35 g if not using the
   vegetable starter culture)
½ sachet vegetable starter culture*
   (this will weigh 1–2 g, depending
   on the brand) (optional)
filtered water (optional)
1 large cabbage leaf, washed

* See Glossary

You'll need a 1.5 litre preserving jar with an airlock lid for this recipe. Wash the jar and all utensils in very hot water or run them through a hot rinse cycle in the dishwasher.

Combine the kohlrabi, radish, peppercorns, bay leaf and spices in a glass or stainless steel bowl. Add the salt and mix well, then cover and set aside.

Dissolve the starter culture (if using) in filtered water according to the packet instructions (the amount of water will depend on the brand you are using). Add to the vegetable mixture and mix well.

Fill the prepared jar with the vegetable mixture, pressing down well with a large spoon or potato masher to remove any air pockets. Leave 2 cm of room free at the top. The vegetables should be completely submerged in the liquid; add more filtered water if necessary.

Take the clean cabbage leaf, fold it up and place it on top of the kohlrabi mixture, then add a small glass weight (a shot glass is ideal) to keep everything submerged. Close the lid, then wrap a tea towel around the jar to block out the light. Store in a dark place (such as an esky) at 16–23°C for 8–15 days (add another 5 days if not using the starter culture). See Notes on page 303 for more information about vegetable culturing times.

Chill before eating. Once opened, the fermented kohlrabi will keep for up to 2 months in the fridge when submerged in the liquid. Unopened, it will keep for up to 9 months in the fridge.

Makes 1 × 1.5 litre jar

I'm sure we have all experienced a time when we have too much cauliflower to get through and we want a bit of a change. This is when fermenting cauliflower comes in handy. It is actually one of my favourite ways to eat it, as it is delicious as well as being amazing for our gut flora. I like a bit of spice with mine, but feel free to omit the chilli if you want something a little more family friendly.

CULTURED CAULIFLOWER AND CELERY

½ head of cauliflower (about 500 g),
    cut into small florets
80 g pomegranate seeds
1 green apple, cored and cut
    into matchsticks
2 celery stalks, sliced
2 celery hearts, including leaves, sliced
160 g fennel, sliced
2 garlic cloves, finely chopped
2 long red chillies, sliced
finely grated zest and juice of 1 lime
1½ teaspoons sea salt
    (or 1 tablespoon if not using the
    vegetable starter culture)
½ sachet vegetable starter culture*
    (this will weigh 1–2 g, depending
    on the brand) (optional)
filtered water (optional)
1 large cabbage leaf, washed

* See Glossary

You'll need a 1.5 litre preserving jar with an airlock lid for this recipe. Wash the jar and all utensils in very hot water or run them through a hot rinse cycle in the dishwasher.

Place the cauliflower, pomegranate seeds, apple, celery, celery heart, fennel, garlic, chilli and lime zest and juice in a glass or stainless steel bowl and sprinkle on the salt. Mix well, cover and set aside. If you're only using salt and not the starter culture, massage the vegetables with the salt for 10 minutes to release the liquid. Do not discard the liquid as it will need to be added to the jar for the fermentation process.

Dissolve the starter culture (if using) in filtered water according to the packet instructions (the amount of water will depend on the brand you are using). Add to the cauliflower mixture and mix well.

Fill the prepared jar with the cauliflower mixture and press down with a large spoon to remove any air pockets. Leave 2 cm of room free at the top. The vegetables should be completely submerged in the liquid; add more filtered water if necessary.

Take the cabbage leaf, fold it up and place it on top of the cauliflower mixture, then add a small glass weight (a shot glass is ideal) to keep everything submerged. Close the lid and wrap a tea towel around the jar to block out the light. Store in a dark place (such as an esky) at 16–23°C for 8–15 days (add another 5 days if not using the starter culture). See Notes on the opposite page for more information about vegetable culturing times.

Chill before eating. Once opened, the fermented cauliflower will keep for up to 2 months in the fridge when submerged in the liquid. If unopened, it will keep for up to 9 months in the fridge.

Notes

- Different vegetables have different culturing times and the warmer the climate is, the shorter the time needed. The highest level of good bacteria usually occurs at 8–15 days of fermentation. It's up to you how long you leave it – from as little as 4 days up to a couple of months. Some people prefer the tangier flavour that comes with extra fermenting time.
- Remember never to heat your ferments as they are a live food and heat destroys the beneficial bacteria.
- Start off small with only a teaspoon and work your way up to 1–2 tablespoons per meal a day.

Makes 1 × 1 litre jar

At every meal we serve a type of kraut, kimchi or coconut yoghurt, as we love to incorporate cultured foods to promote beneficial gut bacteria and to help break down the proteins we consume. Autumn kraut, which we sometimes call 'family kraut', is a lovely combination of a few ingredients that pretty much go with anything. This is one dish of fermented goodness the whole family will enjoy. It was taught to me by the fermenting queen, Kitsa Yanniotis of Kitsa's Kitchen. Thanks, Kitsa x

KITSA'S AUTUMN KRAUT

120 g sweet potato, cut into 2 mm strips
120 g carrot, cut into 2 mm matchsticks
120 g turnip, cut into 2 mm matchsticks
120 g radishes, cut into 2 mm slices
120 g beetroot, cut into 2 mm matchsticks
120 g daikon, cut into 2 mm matchsticks
1 large handful of flat-leaf parsley leaves, chopped
1½ teaspoons sea salt (or 3 teaspoons if not using the vegetable starter culture)
½ sachet vegetable starter culture* (this will weigh 1–2 g, depending on the brand) (optional)
filtered water (optional)
1 large cabbage leaf, washed

* See Glossary

You'll need a 1 litre preserving jar with an airlock lid for this recipe. Wash the jar and all utensils in very hot water or run them through a hot rinse cycle in the dishwasher.

Place the sweet potato, carrot, turnip, radish, beetroot, daikon and parsley in a large glass or stainless steel bowl and toss. Sprinkle over the salt, mix well, cover and set aside. If you're only using salt and not the starter culture, massage the vegetables with the salt for 10 minutes to release the liquid. Do not discard the liquid as it will need to be added to the jar for the fermentation process.

Dissolve the starter culture (if using) in filtered water according to the packet instructions (the amount of water will depend on the brand). Add to the vegetable mixture and mix again.

Fill the prepared jar with the vegetable mixture, pressing down well with a large spoon or potato masher to remove any air pockets. Leave 2 cm of room free at the top. The vegetable mixture should be completely submerged in the liquid; add more filtered water if necessary.

Take the cabbage leaf, fold it up and place it on top of the kraut mixture, then add a small glass weight (a shot glass is ideal) to keep everything submerged. Close the lid, then wrap a tea towel around the side of the jar to block out the light. Store the jar in a dark place (such as an esky) at 16–23°C for 8–15 days (add another 5 days if not using the starter culture). See Notes on page 303 for more information about vegetable culturing times.

Chill before eating. Once opened, the kraut will keep for up to 2 months in the fridge when submerged in the liquid. Unopened, it will keep for up to 9 months in the fridge.

I always like to add some spicy fermented goodness to dishes that need a bit of a kick. My kick-ass kimchi will become a favourite, I am sure, when served alongside eggs in the morning or fish or meat and veggies at lunch or dinner. This recipe also has the added benefit of fermented turmeric, which is one ingredient our bodies love to use to maintain great health.

KICK-ASS TURMERIC KIMCHI

500 g Chinese cabbage (wombok)
½ large daikon (about 340 g),
    cut into 2 mm matchsticks
1 red onion, sliced
1 tablespoon finely grated ginger
2 garlic cloves, sliced
2 long red chillies, sliced
1½ teaspoons sea salt
    (or 1 tablespoon if not using the
    vegetable starter culture)
2 teaspoons ground turmeric
2 tablespoons fish sauce
½ sachet vegetable starter culture*
    (this will weigh 1–2 g, depending
    on the brand) (optional)
filtered water (optional)

* See Glossary

You'll need a 1.5 litre preserving jar with an airlock lid for this recipe. Wash the jar and all utensils in very hot water or run them through a hot rinse cycle in the dishwasher.

Remove the outer leaves of the cabbage. Choose one, wash it well and set aside. Shred the remaining cabbage and place it in a large glass or stainless steel bowl.

Add the daikon, onion, ginger, garlic and chilli to the cabbage in the bowl, sprinkle on the salt and mix well. Add the turmeric and fish sauce and mix well, then cover and set aside. If you're only using salt and not the starter culture, massage the vegetables with the salt for 10 minutes to release the liquid. Do not discard the liquid as it will need to be added to the jar for the fermentation process.

Dissolve the starter culture (if using) in filtered water according to the packet instructions (the amount of water will depend on the brand). Add to the vegetables and mix well.

Fill the prepared jar with the vegetable mixture, pressing down well with a large spoon or potato masher to remove any air pockets. Leave 2 cm of room free at the top. The vegetables should be completely submerged in the liquid; add more filtered water if necessary.

Fold the clean cabbage leaf, place it on top of the cabbage mixture and add a small glass weight (a shot glass is ideal) to keep everything submerged. Close the lid, then wrap a tea towel around the side of the jar to block out the light. Store in a dark place (such as an esky) at 16–23°C for 8–15 days (add another 5 days if not using the starter culture). See Notes on page 303 for more information about vegetable culturing times.

Chill before eating. Once opened, the kimchi will keep for up to 2 months in the fridge when submerged in the liquid. Unopened, it will keep for up to 9 months in the fridge.

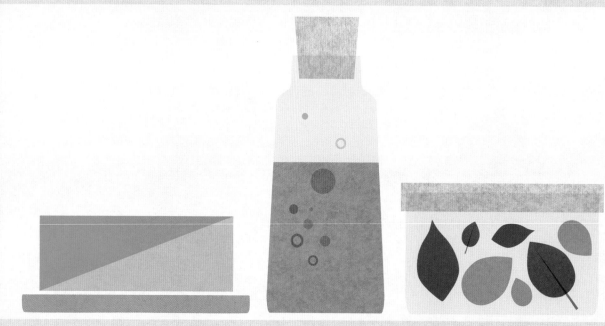

Basics

AIOLI

Makes 470 g
4 Garlic Confit cloves (page 318)
4 egg yolks
2 teaspoons Dijon mustard
2 teaspoons apple cider vinegar
2 tablespoons lemon juice
420 ml (1 ⅔ cups) olive oil
sea salt and freshly ground black pepper

Place the garlic, egg yolks, mustard, vinegar and
lemon juice in the bowl of a food processor and whiz
until combined. With the motor running, slowly pour
in the oil in a thin stream and process until the aioli
is thick and creamy.

Season with salt and pepper. Store in an airtight
container in the fridge for up to 5 days.

BEEF BONE BROTH

Makes 3.5–4 litres
about 2 kg beef knuckle and marrow bones
1 calf foot, chopped into pieces (optional)
3 tablespoons apple cider vinegar
1.5 kg meaty beef rib or neck bones
3 onions, roughly chopped
3 carrots, roughly chopped
3 celery stalks, roughly chopped
2 leeks, white part only, roughly chopped
3 thyme sprigs
2 bay leaves
1 teaspoon black peppercorns, crushed
1 garlic bulb, halved horizontally
2 large handfuls of flat-leaf parsley stalks

Place the knuckle and marrow bones and calf foot
(if using) in a stockpot, add the vinegar and pour in
5 litres of cold water, or enough to cover. Set aside
for 1 hour to help draw out the nutrients from the
bones. Remove the bones from the water, reserving
the water.

Preheat the oven to 180°C (160°C fan-forced). →

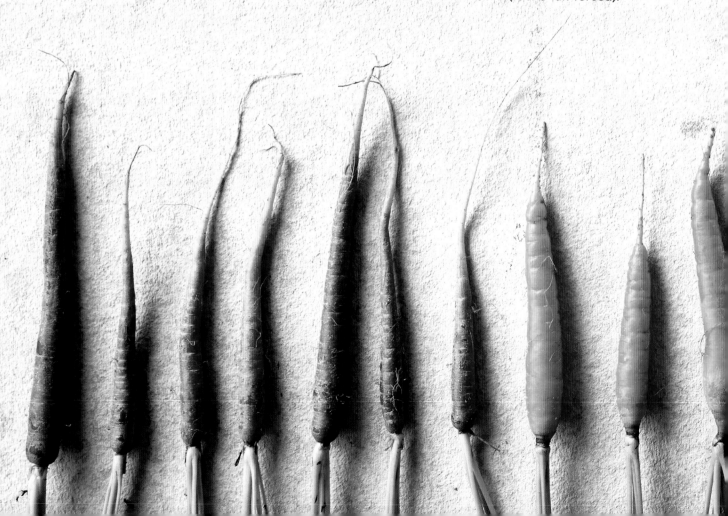

→ Place the knuckle and marrow bones, calf foot (if using) and meaty bones in a few large roasting tins and roast for 30–40 minutes, or until well browned. Return all the bones to the pot and add the vegetables.

Pour the fat from the roasting tins into a saucepan and add 1 litre of the reserved water. Place over high heat and bring to a simmer, stirring with a wooden spoon to loosen any coagulated juices. Add this liquid to the bones and vegetables. If necessary, add the remaining reserved water to the pot to just cover the bones – the liquid should come no higher than 2 cm below the rim of the pot, as the volume will increase slightly during cooking.

Bring the broth to the boil, skimming off the scum that rises to the top. Reduce the heat to low and add the thyme, bay leaves, peppercorns and garlic. Simmer for 12–24 hours. Just before finishing, add the parsley and simmer for 10 minutes. Strain the broth into a large container, discarding the solids, then cover and place in the fridge overnight. Remove the congealed fat that rises to the top (store it in a glass jar in the fridge for up to 2 weeks and use it for frying and sautéing). Transfer the broth to smaller airtight containers and store in the fridge for up to 4 days or freeze for up to 3 months.

CASHEW 'CHEESE'

Makes 220 g
155 g (1 cup) cashew nuts
3 teaspoons lemon juice, plus exra if needed
½ teaspoon sea salt, plus extra if needed
pinch of freshly ground black pepper

Soak the cashews in 750 ml (3 cups) of water for 1–4 hours. Drain and rinse well. Place the cashews in the bowl of a food processor, add the lemon juice, salt and pepper and pulse for 1 minute to combine. Add 3 tablespoons of water and continue to process until smooth. Add a little more lemon juice and salt to taste, if desired. Store in an airtight glass container in the fridge for up to 7 days.

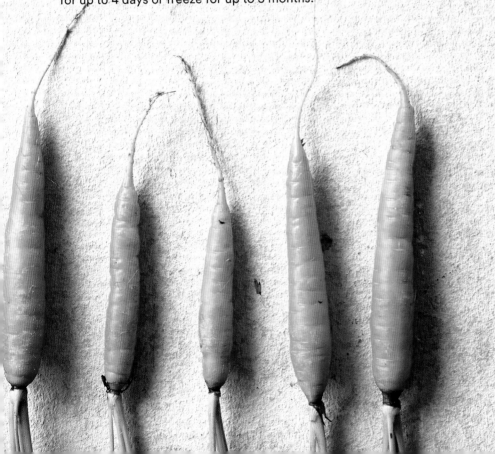

CAULIFLOWER RICE

Serves 4–6

1 head of cauliflower (about 1 kg),
    florets and stalk roughly chopped
2 tablespoons coconut oil
sea salt and freshly ground black pepper

Place the cauliflower in the bowl of a food processor and pulse into tiny, fine pieces that look like rice.

Melt the coconut oil in a large frying pan over medium heat. Add the cauliflower and cook, stirring occasionally, for 3–4 minutes, or until softened. Season with salt and pepper. The cauliflower rice is best eaten straight away, but it can be stored in an airtight container in the fridge for up to 4 days.

CHICKEN BONE BROTH

Makes 3.5 litres

1.5–2 kg bony chicken parts (I like to use necks,
    backs, breastbones and wings)
2–4 chicken feet (optional)
2 tablespoons apple cider vinegar
1 large onion, roughly chopped
2 carrots, roughly chopped
3 celery stalks, roughly chopped
2 leeks, white part only, roughly chopped
1 garlic bulb, halved horizontally
1 tablespoon black peppercorns, lightly crushed
2 bay leaves
2 large handfuls of flat-leaf parsley stalks

Place all the ingredients in a stockpot, add 5 litres of cold water and let stand for 1 hour to help draw out the nutrients from the chicken bones.

Place the pot over medium–high heat and bring to the boil, skimming off the scum that forms on the surface of the liquid. Reduce the heat to low and simmer for 12–24 hours. The longer you cook the broth, the richer and more flavourful it will be.

Strain the broth into a large storage container, cover and place in the fridge overnight. Skim off the congealed fat that rises to the top (store it in a glass jar in the fridge for up to 2 weeks and use it for frying and sautéing). Transfer the broth to smaller airtight containers and store in the fridge for up to 4 days or freeze for up to 3 months.

COCONUT FLOUR PITA BREADS

Makes 8
3 tablespoons coconut flour
3 tablespoons arrowroot*
2 tablespoons almond meal
¼ teaspoon ground turmeric
½ teaspoon fine sea salt
8 large egg whites
2 tablespoons coconut oil

* See Glossary

Whisk the coconut flour, arrowroot, almond meal, turmeric, salt, egg whites and 125 ml (½ cup) of water in a large bowl to make a smooth batter.

Melt 1 teaspoon of oil in a small frying pan over medium–high heat. Pour about 3 tablespoons of batter into the pan. Slightly tilt the pan to swirl and spread out the batter to form a thin round about 13 cm in diameter. Cook for 2 minutes, or until golden brown, then flip and cook the other side until lightly golden. Transfer the pita bread to a plate and keep warm. Repeat until you have used all the batter.

Store in an airtight container in the fridge for up to 1 week or freeze for up to 3 months.

COCONUT YOGHURT

Makes about 1.3 kg
3 tablespoons filtered water
1 tablespoon powdered gelatine*
1.2 litres coconut cream
1–2 tablespoons honey, maple syrup or coconut sugar
4 probiotic capsules* or ¼ teaspoon vegetable
    starter culture*
1 tablespoon lemon juice (optional)

* See Glossary

You'll need a 1.5 litre preserving jar with a lid for this recipe. Wash the jar and all utensils in very hot water or run them through a hot rinse cycle in the dishwasher.

Place the water in a small bowl, sprinkle over the gelatine and soak for 2 minutes. Place the coconut cream in a saucepan and gently heat, stirring with a spoon over medium–low heat until just starting to simmer (90°C, if testing with a thermometer). Do not allow it to boil. Immediately remove the pan from the heat. While still hot, mix in the gelatine mixture, then add the sweetener and mix well. Cover the pan with a lid and set aside to cool to lukewarm (35°C or less). Pour 125 ml (½ cup) of the cooled coconut cream mixture into a sterilised bowl. Open the probiotic capsules (if using). Stir the probiotic powder or starter culture and lemon juice (if using) into the coconut cream in the bowl. Add the remaining coconut cream and mix well. →

→ Pour the coconut cream mixture into the prepared jar and loosely seal the lid. Ferment in a warm spot for 12 hours at 38–40°C. To maintain this temperature and allow the yoghurt to culture, wrap the jar in a tea towel and place it on a plate in the oven with the door shut and the oven light on. The light's warmth will keep the temperature consistent. Alternatively, place the tea-towel-wrapped jar in an esky, fill a heatproof container with boiling water and place it beside the jar – do not allow them to touch – and close the lid. Replace the boiling water halfway through the fermenting process. Once fermented, the yoghurt tends to form air bubbles and looks as though it has separated. Stir well and refrigerate for at least 5 hours before eating. If the yoghurt separates after chilling, give it a good whisk. Store in the fridge for up to 2 weeks.

CRISPY CURRY LEAVES

Makes 4 sprigs
150 ml melted coconut oil
4 curry leaves sprigs
sea salt

Heat the coconut oil in a frying pan over medium heat. Add two sprigs at a time and fry the curry leaves for 4–5 seconds, or until crisp. Remove with a slotted spoon, drain on paper towel and season with salt. Repeat with the remaining sprigs.

CRISPY GARLIC

Makes 3–4 tablespoons
6 garlic cloves, thinly sliced
250 ml (1 cup) melted coconut oil

Place the garlic and oil in a saucepan and heat over medium heat for about 5 minutes, or until the garlic starts to turn golden. Lift out the garlic with a slotted spoon and drain on paper towel. The coconut oil will have taken on a lovely garlicky flavour and you can use it for sautéing vegetables or cooking meat, chicken or fish. Store the crispy garlic in an airtight container in the pantry for up to 1 week.

DASHI BROTH

Makes 1.4 litres
3 dried kombu sheets* (each 15 cm × 11 cm)
50 g (2 heaped cups) bonito flakes*
1 teaspoon sea salt
1½ teaspoons tamari or coconut aminos*

* See Glossary

Cut small slits in the kombu with a pair of scissors or tear with your hands to help release the flavour. Place the kombu and 1.5 litres of water in a large saucepan and set aside to soak until the kombu starts to soften – about 1 hour.

Place the pan over medium–low heat and bring to a gentle simmer (ideally 60–71°C), making sure that the water does not boil. (Boiling the kombu gives the dashi an intense flavour and turns the broth cloudy. Cooking the kombu at a lower temperature yields a clearer broth.) Cook gently for 1 hour, or until the kombu is tender enough to be pierced easily with a chopstick and the broth has a mild sea-like aroma and a noticeable but delicate salty flavour. Strain the broth, discarding the kombu.

Return the broth to the pan and warm over medium–low heat until steam rises from the surface of the liquid (about 85°C). Add the bonito flakes and salt and push down gently with a spoon to submerge the flakes – you do not want to break up the fine pieces. Turn off the heat and let the bonito flakes steep in the hot broth for 5 minutes.

Strain the dashi broth through a fine sieve into a jug, taking care not to squeeze or press the flakes. Discard the bonito flakes.

Season the dashi with the tamari or coconut aminos. If not using immediately, let the dashi cool at room temperature for about 30 minutes until lukewarm, then refrigerate, uncovered, until completely cool. Cover and refrigerate for up to 3 days or freeze for up to 3 months.

DYNAMITE SAUCE

Makes 170 g
150 g Mayonnaise (page 320)
1–2 tablespoons sriracha sauce, or to taste
¼ teaspoon toasted sesame oil

Whisk all the ingredients in a bowl until well blended. Store in an airtight container in the fridge for up to 2 weeks.

Tip
– You can use the equivalent amount of tabasco, sambal or chilli oil/flakes instead of the sriracha sauce if you prefer.

FISH BONE BROTH

Makes about 3 litres

2 tablespoons coconut oil
2 celery stalks, roughly chopped
2 onions, roughly chopped
1 carrot, roughly chopped
125 ml (½ cup) dry white wine or vermouth (optional)
3 or 4 non-oily fish carcasses and heads
    (such as snapper, barramundi or kingfish)
3 tablespoons apple cider vinegar
1 handful of thyme and flat-leaf parsley sprigs
1 bay leaf

Melt the oil in a stockpot or large saucepan over medium–low heat. Add the vegetables and cook gently for 30–60 minutes, or until soft. Pour in the wine or vermouth (if using) and bring to the boil. Add the fish carcasses and cover with 3.5 litres of cold water. Stir in the vinegar and bring to the boil, skimming off the scum and any impurities as they rise to the top.

Tie the herbs together with kitchen string and add to the broth. Reduce the heat to low, cover and simmer for at least 3 hours. Remove the fish carcasses and herbs with tongs or a slotted spoon and strain the broth into storage containers. Cover and refrigerate overnight. Remove the congealed fat that rises to the top. (Store it in a glass jar in the fridge for up to 2 weeks and use it for frying and sautéing.) Store the broth in the fridge for up to 4 days or in the freezer for up to 3 months.

FURIKAKE SEASONING

Makes 30 g

2 nori sheets*, torn or snipped into 3 cm pieces
2 teaspoons sea salt
3 tablespoons bonito flakes*
pinch of coconut sugar (optional)
1½ tablespoons sesame seeds, toasted

* See Glossary

Place the nori, salt and bonito flakes in a blender and pulse a few times to finely chop the nori. Mix in the sugar (if using) and toasted sesame seeds and set aside until needed. Store in an airtight container in the pantry for up to 3 months.

GARLIC CONFIT

Makes 25 cloves

25 garlic cloves, peeled
250 ml (1 cup) melted coconut oil

Place the garlic and oil in a saucepan over very low heat (do not allow the oil to boil). Gently poach for 1 hour, or until the garlic is beautifully soft. Transfer the garlic and oil to a sterilised glass jar (see page 314 for instructions), seal and store in the fridge for up to 3 months.

GREEN CURRY PASTE

Makes 300 g

4 kaffir lime leaves, finely chopped
2 red Asian shallots, chopped
3 garlic cloves, chopped
1 tablespoon chopped coriander roots and stalks
1.5 cm piece of galangal, peeled and finely chopped
1 lemongrass stem, pale part only, finely chopped
1.5 cm piece of ginger, peeled and finely chopped
1 teaspoon finely grated fresh turmeric or
    ½ teaspoon dried turmeric
4 long green chillies, halved, deseeded and sliced
2 small green chillies, sliced
1 teaspoon roasted shrimp paste
finely grated zest of ½ lime
1½ teaspoons ground coriander
1½ teaspoons ground cumin
pinch of freshly ground black pepper
½ teaspoon sea salt
2 tablespoons coconut oil

Place all the ingredients in the bowl of a food processor and blitz to a fine paste. Add 3 tablespoons of water and process to combine. Store in a sealed container in the fridge for up to 1 month.

ITALIAN TOMATO SAUCE

Makes 700 g

2 tablespoons coconut oil or good-quality animal fat*
1 onion, chopped
6 garlic cloves, thinly sliced
800 g whole peeled tomatoes, crushed (see Note page 48)
sea salt and freshly ground black pepper

Heat the oil or fat in a saucepan over medium heat, add the onion and cook, stirring occasionally, for 5 minutes, or until translucent. Stir in the garlic and cook for 1 minute, or until the garlic is fragrant. Add the tomatoes and 125 ml (½ cup) of water and simmer for 25–30 minutes, or until reduced and thickened. Season to taste, transfer to a blender and blend until smooth. Store in a glass jar in the fridge for up to 2 weeks.

JAPANESE MAYONNAISE

Makes about 500 g

4 egg yolks
2 teaspoons Dijon mustard
1½ tablespoon apple cider vinegar
1 teaspoon tamari or coconut aminos*
¼ teaspoon garlic powder
400 ml olive oil or macadamia oil, or 200 ml of each
sea salt and freshly ground black pepper

* See Glossary

Place the egg yolks, mustard, vinegar, tamari or coconut aminos, garlic powder, oil and a pinch of salt in a glass jug or jar and blend with a hand-held blender until smooth and creamy. Season with salt and pepper.

Alternatively, place the egg yolks, mustard, vinegar, tamari or coconut aminos, garlic powder and a pinch of salt in the bowl of a food processor and process until combined. With the motor running, slowly pour in the oil in a thin stream and process until the mayonnaise is thick and creamy. Season with salt and pepper.

Store in a sealed glass jar in the fridge for up to 5 days.

MACADAMIA 'CHEESE'

Makes about 600 g
320 g macadamia nuts
1–1½ tablespoons lemon juice
1 teaspoon sea salt, plus extra if needed
pinch of freshly ground black pepper

Soak the macadamia nuts in 750 ml (3 cups) of water for 6 hours. Drain and rinse well. Place the nuts in the bowl of a food processor, add the lemon juice, salt and pepper and pulse for 1 minute to combine. Add 120 ml of water and process until smooth. If it seems a little dry, add more water and lemon juice to adjust the consistency. Store in an airtight container in the fridge for up to 1 week.

MAYONNAISE

Makes about 500 g
4 egg yolks
2 teaspoons Dijon mustard
1 tablespoon apple cider vinegar
1 tablespoon lemon juice
400 ml olive oil or macadamia oil, or 200 ml of each
sea salt and freshly ground black pepper

Place the egg yolks, mustard, vinegar, lemon juice, oil and a pinch of salt in a glass jug or jar and blend with a hand-held blender until smooth and creamy. Season with salt and pepper.

Alternatively, place the egg yolks, mustard, vinegar, lemon juice and a pinch of salt in the bowl of a food processor and process until combined. With the motor running, slowly pour in the oil in a thin stream and process until the mayonnaise is thick and creamy. Season with salt and pepper.

Store in a sealed glass jar in the fridge for up to 5 days.

PALEO BUTTER

Makes 240 g
2 tablespoons coconut cream
80 ml (⅓ cup) melted coconut oil
125 ml (½ cup) olive oil or macadamia oil
½ teaspoon sea salt

Place all the ingredients in a blender and blend until creamy. Pour into a small glass container with a lid, cover and refrigerate for 4 hours, or until set. Store in the fridge until needed.

PICKLED RADISH

Makes 1 × 500 ml jar
200 ml apple cider vinegar
3 tablespoons honey
½ teaspoon sea salt
½ teaspoon black peppercorns
2 bay leaves
100 ml filtered water, plus extra if needed
10 radishes, quartered

You will need a 500 ml (2 cup) glass jar with an airtight lid for this recipe. Wash the jar and all utensils in very hot water or run them through a hot rinse cycle in the dishwasher.

Bring the vinegar, honey, salt, peppercorns, bay leaves and filtered water to the boil in a small saucepan. Add the radish quarters and set aside to cool. Place the radish and the pickling liquid in the prepared jar. The vegetables should be completely submerged in the liquid; if not, add more filtered water to cover. Seal with the lid and refrigerate for 3 days before using. The pickled radish will keep for up to 3 weeks in the fridge.

PUMPKIN PUREE

Makes 550 g

700 g butternut or kent pumpkin, peeled
and cut into 3 cm chunks

Preheat the oven to 180°C (160°C fan-forced).

Place the pumpkin in a casserole dish and pour in
3 tablespoons of water. Cover with a lid and bake
for 1 hour, or until very soft and tender. Allow to cool.

Place the cooled pumpkin in the bowl of a food
processor and process until smooth.

Store in a sealed container in the fridge for up
to 10 days.

SAUERKRAUT

Makes 1 × 1.5 litre jar

400 g green cabbage
400 g red cabbage
1 beetroot, peeled
2 carrots (about 250 g in total)
1½ teaspoons sea salt
1 sachet vegetable starter culture*
    (this will weigh 2–5 g, depending on the brand)

* See Glossary

You will need a 1.5 litre preserving jar with an airlock
lid for this recipe. Wash the jar and all utensils
thoroughly in very hot water. Alternatively, run
them through a hot rinse cycle in the dishwasher.

Remove the outer leaves of the cabbages. Choose
an unblemished leaf, wash it well and set aside.

Shred the cabbages, beetroot and carrot in a food
processor or slice with a knife or mandoline, then
transfer to a large glass bowl. Sprinkle over the salt,
mix well and cover with a plate.

Prepare the starter culture according to the
directions on the packet. Add to the cabbage
mixture and mix thoroughly.

Fill the prepared jar with the cabbage mix, pressing
down well with a large spoon to remove any air
pockets. Leave 2 cm of room free at the top. The
cabbage mixture should be completely submerged
in its juices; add some filtered water if necessary.

Take the clean reserved cabbage leaf, fold it up
and place it on top of the cabbage mix, then add
a small glass weight (a shot glass is ideal) to keep
everything submerged. Close the lid. Wrap a tea
towel around the side of the jar to block out the
light. Store in a dark place (such as an esky) at
16–23°C for 10–14 days.

Chill before eating. Once opened, the kraut will keep
for up to 2 months in the fridge when submerged in
liquid. If unopened, it will keep for up to 9 months in
the fridge. Don't throw out the brine – it can be used
for a delicious dressing.

SEMI-DRIED TOMATOES

Makes 350 g

500 g roma or truss tomatoes, cut into 2.5 cm wedges
sea salt and freshly ground black pepper
1½ teaspoons dried oregano
100 ml extra-virgin olive oil

Preheat the oven to 120°C (100°C fan-forced).
Line a baking tray with baking paper and place
a wire rack on the tray.

Arrange the tomatoes, cut-side up, on the wire
rack. Season the tomatoes with salt and pepper
and sprinkle on the dried oregano. Bake for 2 hours,
or until the tomatoes are dry around the edges but
still soft in the centre. Set aside to cool completely.
Transfer the tomatoes to a sterilised glass jar (see
page 314 for instructions), pour in the olive oil, seal
and store in the fridge for up to 2 weeks.

TERIYAKI SAUCE

Makes 200 ml
125 ml (½ cup) tamari or coconut aminos*
3 tablespoons coconut sugar
3 tablespoons honey
2 teaspoons finely grated garlic
1 teaspoon finely grated ginger
1½ teaspoons tapioca flour*

* See Glossary

Mix the tamari or coconut aminos, sugar, honey, garlic, ginger and 3 tablespoons of water in a small saucepan and place over medium heat. Bring to the boil, then reduce the heat to low and gently simmer for 5 minutes to dissolve the sugar and allow the flavours to develop.

Meanwhile, mix the tapioca flour and 1 tablespoon of water until combined.

Bring the tamari mixture to the boil, then pour in the tapioca mixture. Stir constantly until the sauce coats the back of the spoon. Remove from the heat. Allow to cool, then strain, discarding the ginger and garlic pulp. Store in an airtight glass bottle in the fridge for up to 4 weeks.

TOASTED SPICED SEEDS

Makes about 60 g
3 tablespoons pumpkin seeds (activated if possible*)
3 tablespoons sunflower seeds (activated if possible*)
1 tablespoon za'atar*
1 tablespoon olive oil
pinch of sea salt

* See Glossary

Preheat the oven to 160°C (140°C fan-forced). Line a baking tray with baking paper.

Mix all the ingredients together to combine.

Spread the seed mixture over the prepared tray in a single layer and bake for 10–12 minutes, or until golden. Allow to cool on the tray. Store in an airtight container in the pantry for up to 3 months.

WHIPPED COCONUT CREAM

Makes 750 ml
800 ml coconut cream
2 tablespoons honey, or to taste

Place the unopened container/s of coconut cream in a stainless steel bowl and refrigerate overnight.

Open the container/s of chilled coconut cream and scoop the contents into another bowl. Separate the hardened cream layer from the water layer. Place the cream layer and the honey in the chilled bowl. (Store the coconut water in a sealed container in the fridge for another use.)

Use an electric mixer to whip the coconut cream and honey on high speed for about 3 minutes, or until soft peaks form. Allow to set for 40 minutes in the fridge before using.

GLOSSARY

ACTIVATED CHARCOAL

Activated charcoal is made from slowly burnt wood, peat or coconut shells treated with oxygen. What is left is a charcoal that is highly porous and is able to adsorb or bind to toxins and odours and expel them from the body. The powder is tasteless and odourless.

ACTIVATED NUTS AND SEEDS

Nuts and seeds are a great source of healthy fats, but they contain phytic acid, which binds to minerals so that they can't be readily absorbed. Activating nuts and seeds lessens the phytates, making minerals easier to absorb. Activated nuts and seeds are available from health-food stores. To make your own, simply soak the nuts in filtered water (12 hours for hard nuts, such as almonds; 4–6 hours for seeds and softer nuts, such as cashews). Rinse the nuts, then spread out on a baking tray and place in a 50°C oven or dehydrator to dry out. This will take anywhere from 6 to 24 hours, depending on the temperature and the nuts or seeds. Store in an airtight container in the pantry for up to 3 months.

ALOE VERA JUICE

Aloe vera juice is a gooey, thick liquid made from the flesh of the aloe vera plant leaf. Aloe vera juice is very mild and can be added to smoothies. It is thought to aid digestion and boost the immune system.

ARROWROOT

Arrowroot is a starch made from the roots of several tropical plants. In Australia, arrowroot and tapioca flour are considered the same, even though they are actually from different plants. It can be found at health-food stores and some supermarkets.

BAHARAT

Baharat is a Middle Eastern spice blend that includes black pepper, coriander seeds, paprika, cardamom, nutmeg, cumin, cloves and cinnamon. It is great for seasoning meats and vegetables, adding to dips and sauces, or using as a dry rub or marinade for veggies, meat – especially lamb and poultry – and fish. Look for baharat at Middle Eastern grocers, delis and some supermarkets.

BONITO FLAKES

Bonito flakes are made from the bonito fish, which is like a small tuna. The fish is smoked, fermented, dried and shaved, and the end product looks similar to wood shavings. Bonito flakes are used to garnish Japanese dishes, to make sauces such as ponzu, soups such as miso, and to make the Japanese stock, dashi. You can find bonito flakes in Asian food stores.

COCONUT AMINOS

Made from coconut sap, coconut aminos is similar in flavour to a light soy sauce. Because it is free of both soy and gluten, it makes a great paleo alternative to soy sauce and tamari. Coconut aminos is available at health-food stores or online.

CONCENTRATED PROBIOTIC POWDER

Adding probiotic powder to your diet can have positive health benefits. Probiotics are live bacteria and yeasts that are good for your health, especially your digestive system. We usually think of bacteria as germs that lead to illness. But your body is full of both good and bad bacteria. Probiotics keep your gut healthy by promoting good bacteria.

EGGSHELL CALCIUM POWDER

Eggshell calcium powder is a natural source of calcium and other elements. It has positive effects on bone and cartilage and can be used in the prevention and treatment of osteoporosis. Make sure you source your eggshell calcium from pastured hens.

GELATINE

Gelatine is the cooked form of collagen, which is a protein found in bones, skin and connective tissue. I always choose gelatine sourced from organic, grass-fed beef, such as Great Lakes Gelatin Company. Vegetarian substitutes for gelatine include agar agar and carrageen, which are made from two different types of seaweed. Sometimes these aren't as strong as regular gelatine, so you may need to increase the quantity. Some kosher gelatines are also vegan. You can buy gelatine made from organic, grass-fed beef, agar agar and carrageen from health-food stores or online.

GOOD-QUALITY ANIMAL FAT

I use either coconut oil or good-quality animal fats for cooking as they have high smoke points (meaning they do not oxidise at high temperatures). Some of my favourite animal fats to use are lard (pork fat), tallow (rendered beef fat), rendered chicken fat and duck fat. These may be hard to find – ask at your local butcher or meat supplier, look online for meat **suppliers who sell them, or make your own when making bone broths.**

KOMBU

Kombu is a high-protein sea vegetable, rich in calcium, iron, iodine and dietary fibre. It is salty and savoury and plays a vital role in Japanese cuisine. Kombu can be used in a similar way to bay leaves – add them to a stew or curry for a flavour boost and remove them after cooking. Kombu can be found in Asian grocers and is mainly sold dried or pickled in vinegar. Dried kombu is often covered with a white powder from natural salts and starch. It is harmless but can easily be removed with a damp cloth.

KOREAN CHILLI POWDER (GOCHUGARU)

Korean chilli powder is made from thin red chillies that are dried in the sun and ground. It has smoky, fruity sweet notes, with a hot kick, and is used to make classic Korean dishes such as kimchi and bulgogi. It is also great for stir-fries, dipping sauces and meat marinades. You can find Korean chilli powder in Asian supermarkets.

MCT OIL

MCTs are medium-chain triglycerides, a form of saturated fatty acid that has numerous health benefits, ranging from improved cognitive function to better weight management. MCTs get their name from their chemical structure. Compared with longer-chained fats, MCTs permeate the cells and are easily digestible.

MUSHROOM POWDER

Mushroom powder is used to support the immune system and reduce inflammation and signs of ageing. It is also used to protect the liver and other organs from free radicals due to its high antioxidant content.

NORI SHEETS

Nori is a dark green, paper-like, toasted seaweed used in Japanese dishes. Nori provides an abundance of essential nutrients and is rich in vitamins, iron and other minerals, amino acids, omega-3 and omega-6, and antioxidants. Nori sheets are commonly used to roll sushi, but they can also be added to salads, soups and many other dishes. You can buy nori sheets from Asian grocers and most supermarkets.

NUTRITIONAL YEAST FLAKES

Nutritional yeast is a source of complete protein and vitamins, in particular B-complex vitamins. It contains thiamine, folates, niacin, selenium, zinc and riboflavin, making it highly nutritious.

PROBIOTIC CAPSULES

Probiotic capsules contain live bacteria that can help to regulate digestion, clear up yeast infections and assist with conditions such as irritable bowel syndrome. These capsules need to be kept in the fridge. They can be swallowed whole or opened up and used to ferment drinks and yoghurt. Probiotic capsules can be found at pharmacies and health-food stores.

PSYLLIUM HUSKS

Psyllium, also known as ispaghula, is a gluten-free, soluble fibre produced from the *Plantago ovata* plant, native to India and Pakistan. Psyllium is an indigestible dietary fibre and is primarily used to maintain intestinal health, as the high fibre content absorbs excess liquid in the gut. When exposed to liquids, the husks swell up to create a gel. It is therefore important to drink plenty of fluids when consuming psyllium. Psyllium products can be found at health-food stores and some supermarkets.

RAS EL HANOUT

Ras el hanout, a traditional complex spice blend that translates as 'top of the shop', originates from North Africa and may contain more than 30 spices and herbs. It is used to flavour Moroccan dishes and is great for seasoning fish, chicken and lamb. You can buy it from Middle Eastern grocers, delis and some supermarkets.

SHICHIMI TOGARASHI

Shichimi togarashi literally means 'seven flavour chilli pepper' and is one of the most popular condiments on Japanese tables. As the name suggests, this spice mixture is made from seven ingredients, typically including red chilli, Japanese (sansho) peppers, orange peel, black and white sesame seeds, ginger and seaweed. Apart from the chillies, the ingredients vary, and if you are lucky you may come across a Japanese vendor offering a custom blend.

STEVIA

Native to South America, this herb grows into a shrub with naturally sweet leaves. The sweet extraction has no calories and is over 100 times sweeter than cane sugar so should be used sparingly. Stevia leaves have been used by the people of Brazil and Paraguay for hundreds of years as a means of sweetening food. Stevia is also believed to provide relief from some skin irritations.

SUMAC

Sumac is a spice made from red sumac berries that have been dried and crushed. It has antimicrobial properties and a tangy, lemony flavour, which makes it ideal for pairing with seafood. It's also delicious in salad dressings. You can buy it from Middle Eastern grocers, delis and some supermarkets.

TAPIOCA FLOUR

Tapioca flour is made by grinding up the dried root of the manioc (also known as cassava) plant. It can be used to thicken dishes or in gluten-free baking. You can find tapioca flour at health-food stores and some supermarkets. See also Arrowroot.

VEGETABLE STARTER CULTURE

A vegetable starter culture is a preparation used to kickstart the fermentation process when culturing vegetables and yoghurts. I use a broad-spectrum starter sourced from organic vegetables rather than one grown from dairy sources, as this ensures the highest number of living, active bacteria and produces consistently successful results free of pathogens. Vegetable starter culture usually comes in sachets and can be purchased from health-food stores or online. You can also get fresh, non-dairy starter cultures for yoghurt and kefir (I recommend kulturedwellness.com).

WAKAME

Wakame is an edible seaweed used in Japanese, Korean and Chinese cuisine. It's great in soups, salads and stir-fries. Wakame contains iron, magnesium, iodine, calcium and lignans. You can find it in Asian grocers and some supermarkets.

YUZU JUICE

Yuzu is a Japanese citrus fruit that has an extraordinary spicy citrus flavour, somewhere between a lemon and a lime. Yuzu juice is very high in vitamin C and is great in cocktails, dressings, dips and sashimi dishes. You can buy yuzu juice from Asian grocers.

ZA'ATAR

Za'atar is a Middle Eastern spice mix that is used to flavour meats, seafood, eggs, soups, vegetables and poultry. Za'atar contains thyme, sumac, sesame seeds, oregano, marjoram and salt. You can buy it from Middle Eastern grocers, delis and some supermarkets.

THANKS

A mountain of gratitude to my glorious family, especially my wonderful wife, Nic, and my two amazing daughters, Indii and Chilli. You three angels are a constant source of pure inspiration and happiness, and it is a humbling honour to walk beside you all throughout this life. Thank you for being your bright, fun-loving, authentic and unconditionally loving selves.

To the absolute wonder twins, Monica and Jacinta Cannataci, you both add your own magic essence to everything we create together, and this book just wouldn't be the same without your input. Thank you both for working so graciously and tirelessly, and for all that you do!

To Kylie Bailey, thank you so much for helping get this book to where it is now. So many people will benefit greatly from all your hard work.

To Anthony and Crystal at The Healthy Patch, thanks for all your invaluable gardening advice.

To the incredible photography and styling team of Steve Brown, Jonathan Fleming, Deb Kaloper, Hannah Meppem, William Meppem, Rob Palmer, Mark Roper and Lucy Tweed, you all bring a unique sense of beauty that never ceases to be exceptionally pleasing, and I'm endlessly thankful for you all.

To Ingrid Ohlsson and Mary Small, thank you for passionately orchestrating the path that allows so much goodness to come to life. It is a pleasure to work with you both, always!

Thanks to Clare Marshall, for making sure everything is as it should be. It is a joy to have you crossing the T's and dotting the I's.

To Charlotte Ree, thanks for being the best publicist any author could wish to work with.

To Megan Johnston, thank you for your careful and thorough editing.

To Lucy Sykes-Thompson of Studio Polka, thank you for creating such a gorgeous design for the book.

A very warm thank you to my sweet mum, Joy. Among many things, you passed on your love of cooking and there's no doubt that I wouldn't be where I am without you.

I also wish to express a huge thank you to my teachers, peers, mentors and friends, who are all genuinely working towards creating a healthier world and who are all in their own right true forces for good: Nora Gedgaudas and Lisa Collins, Trevor Hendy, Rudy Eckhardt, Dr Pete Bablis, Dr David Perlmutter, Dr Alessio Fasano, Dr Kelly Brogan, Dr William Davis, Dr Joseph Mercola, Helen Padarin, Dr Natasha Campbell-McBride, Dr Frank Lipman, Dr Libby, Prof. Tim Noakes, Pete Melov and Prof. Martha Herbert, to name a few.

INDEX

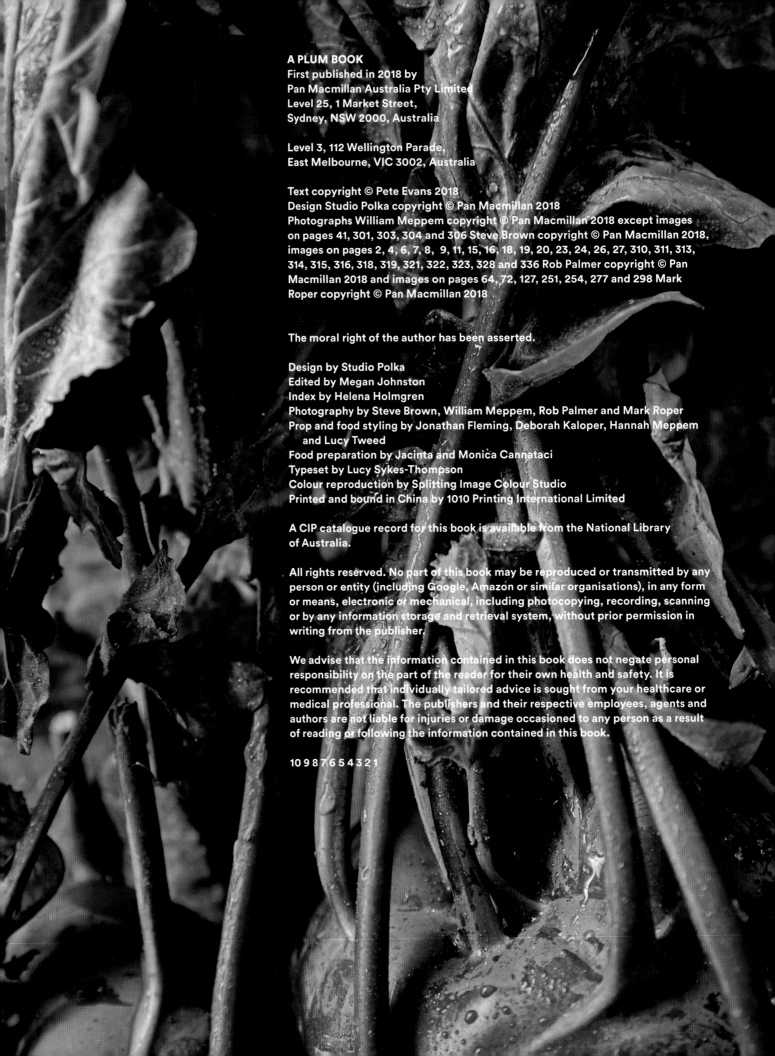

A PLUM BOOK
First published in 2018 by
Pan Macmillan Australia Pty Limited
Level 25, 1 Market Street,
Sydney, NSW 2000, Australia

Level 3, 112 Wellington Parade,
East Melbourne, VIC 3002, Australia

Design by Studio Polka
Edited by Megan Johnston
Index by Helena Holmgren
Photography by Steve Brown, William Meppem, Rob Palmer and Mark Roper
Prop and food styling by Jonathan Fleming, Deborah Kaloper, Hannah Meppem
    and Lucy Tweed
Food preparation by Jacinta and Monica Cannataci
Typeset by Lucy Sykes-Thompson
Colour reproduction by Splitting Image Colour Studio
Printed and bound in China by 1010 Printing International Limited

A CIP catalogue record for this book is available from the National Library
of Australia.

10 9 8 7 6 5 4 3 2 1